The Five Brothers

The Five Brothers: Our Journeys to Successful Careers in Law & Medicine

Phillip Bazemore, JD
F. Travis Buchanan, Esq.
Dr. Neville Campbell
Judge Carlos E. Moore
Charles Tucker, Jr., Esq.

with Mary Flowers Boyce

The Five Brothers: our journeys to successful careers
in law & medicine

Memoir
First Edition
With Mary Flowers Boyce

ISBN Print 978-1-7360775-0-4
ISBN Electronic 978-1-7360775-1-1

Library of Congress Control Number: 2020922230

Table of Contents

Dedication i

Foreword..iii

Preface ix

Introduction..xiii

Chapter 1: Go Daddy.................................. 1

Chapter 2: Mama's Boys 19

Chapter 3: Excellence............................ 35

Chapter 4: Independence Day 40

Chapter 5: South Mississippi Strong 47

Chapter 6: Angels................................. 53

Chapter 7: The Prince of Queens 58

Chapter 8: Rebel with a Cause 67

Chapter 9: The Turning Point 72

Chapter 10: Legacy............................... 79

Reflections 92

Dedication

To my beautiful wife, Natalie, thanks for being my biggest cheerleader and my rock. To my precious daughter, Avery Nicole, you are my greatest inspiration and reason for being. May this book inspire you and your generation to soar like eagles and rise above any obstacles to achieve your dreams. Finally, to my parents, Anthony and Carolyn, thanks for your many sacrifices and most of all, the gift of your love.

Judge Carlos Moore

To LaDonna, Cassidy, Londyn, and Charles III, the true inspirations in my life. And to my Mom and Dad who made sacrifices for me so that I could make my dreams come true. I thank God for you both.

Charles Tucker, Jr

To my three ladies, Carla, Lauren, and Sydney, as it is family that motivates me and keeps me focused.

F. Travis Buchanan

To my Mom, my Dad, my wife Tashi, my three daughters Tashell, Giselle, and Gabrielle, and my brothers and sisters especially Valerie, Stevie, and Eddarine. I would not be the man I am today without your inspiration, guidance, love, and support. Thank You.

Dr. Neville Campbell

To my mother Carmen, my father Warren, my brother Todd, my sisters Jahniya, and Alexis. My family, I cherish and love you dearly.

To Reganel for continuously giving preparation an opportunity. Thank you.

Phillip Bazemore

Foreword

James Baldwin wrote his nephew a letter by which he attempted to convey certain harsh realities of being born male and Black in the United States of America. His warnings, though provided well over fifty years ago—remain as accurate and as powerful as they were when they were first penned. He suggested:

"This innocent country set you down in a ghetto in which, in fact, it intended that you should perish. Let me spell out precisely what I mean by that, for the heart of the matter is here and the crux of my dispute with my country. You were born where you were born and faced the future that you faced because you were Black and for no other reason. The limits to your ambition were thus expected to be settled. You were born into a society which spelled out with brutal clarity and in as many ways as possible that you were a worthless human being. You were not expected to aspire to excellence. You were expected to make peace with mediocrity."

The government sponsored so-called "war on drugs" has evolved into what has effectively become a war on Black and Brown communities. Though these communities are no more drug-ridden than their suburban counterparts, our legal system regularly targets them for campaigns of terror, brutality, incarceration, and violence.

One out of four Black men will lose their freedom and be incarcerated at some point during their lifetime. Black men are 2.5 times more likely to be shot and killed by the police. In a nation that boasts more guns than people, Black men are 15 times more likely to be victims of gun violence. Furthermore, a crisis lack of access to appropriate healthcare has culminated in rising suicide rates among African-American men whose mental health remains undiagnosed, under-treated, and understudied.

This story of five brothers who overcame the odds to achieve careers in law and medicine must be read in the context of an era of mass incarceration and the effective criminalization of blackness itself that characterizes much of the American legal system. There is both pain and pride in knowing that in spite of all that the Five Brothers have accomplished, they are still more likely to become victims of violence than their white counterparts.

As joyous as it is to celebrate their accomplishments, there is a list of young African-American men whose lives were cut short at the hands of the very people whose job it was to protect and serve them.

The Five Brothers' journey to praiseworthy careers in law and medicine should not be an anomaly in this country, and let's hope it is not.

The question becomes, then, why don't we hear more stories of successful Black men who are educated, God-fearing and family-oriented with a mission to mentor others? Is it so uncommon or are they over shadowed by negative images of Black men in media, fiction, music videos, and film?

Each of the five brothers share multiple

depictions of what has gone right and wrong in their lives, with their parents and other mentors being a running topic. There is no wonder that they are so fiercely committed to giving back, and they are savvy enough to recognize that it starts with becoming the best men they can be.

There are lessons about racism, feeling unwanted, colorism, competition, developing confidence and swagger, as well as lessons about love, forgiveness, and fatherhood.

If nothing else, *The Five Brothers: Our Journeys to Careers in Law & Medicine*, points out that there is no singular road map to making it in this country, and there is no singular characteristic that one must possess to achieve great things.

Single-parent and two-parent households, upper class, middle class and poor, public-school and parochial-school educated, Catholic and Protestant, sons of college grads and blue-collar immigrants, born in the U.S. or outside of it, pampered and punished harshly, they run the gamut. There is, in fact, no blueprint.

The one commonality, however, seems to be an expectation of excellence that James Baldwin cautioned his nephew he was not supposed to aspire to, and the good news is that expectation came from parents, teachers, pastors, employers, and even neighbors. If you are any of these things to any boys or girls, your charge is placed before you: Do something to make a child believe that he can be great.

But, of course, the harsh reality that Baldwin

spoke of cannot be escaped.

One of the brothers tells the story that stood out most for me about a violent, harrowing, life-changing encounter he had with a rogue cop in Jacksonville, Florida, proving, yet again, that even when you try to do everything right, for Black men, too often, that isn't enough.

That was true for Botham Jean—a 26-year-old accountant for PWC. He graduated at the top of his class, excelled in his industry, and was committed to the service of others. A police officer entered his Dallas apartment and shot him to death as he sat eating a bowl of ice cream at the end of the day. The officer claimed she entered his apartment mistakenly believing it to be her own, and shot Botham believing him to be an intruder.

It was true for 15-year-old Jordan Edwards. He and his brother were at a party near Dallas, Texas, police arrived after noise complaints and, the two brothers did what their parents had instructed if trouble arose: they left. Jordan, a passenger in a car, was fatally shot in the back of the head by a police officer. There is only one race of teenagers that police feel comfortable enough to fire fatal shots at as they leave a party trying to get home. Jordan, like the Five Brothers, was a good student with a promising future.

It was true of Jemel Roberson who overcame the infamous Southside Chicago streets to work in the ministry and was working to pursue a career in law enforcement. One day while moonlighting as a security guard for a nightclub, he helped disarm a would-be mass shooter who began shooting into a crowd following a dispute with another patron. As he held the shooter down and waited for law enforcement, police arrived and shot him in his back four times, killing him.

In overcoming the odds, the Five Brothers had to navigate the common obstacles and the hurdles unique to the Black experience. Like Atatiana Jefferson of Fort Worth, Texas, these brothers were able to rise above family and community limitations. She, herself, attended an HBCU and was pursuing a career in the medical field. As she balanced her responsibilities at home and her professional pursuits, she always made time to invest in her seven-year-old nephew, Zion. One late Friday night, she and Zion stayed up late playing video games when they heard noises coming from the backyard. When Atatiana went to the window to investigate, she was shot by a Fort Worth police officer through her bedroom window.

State-sanctioned and sponsored violence remains an omnipresence in the Black experience. It cannot be mastered by compliance, model parenting, or even following the straight and narrow path.

So celebrate the Five Brothers, yes, but let's all celebrate with the intention of doing what we can to ensure that much-needed changes are made. If we all commit to doing this, more Black men can live out their dreams, or at least make it home.

Lee Merritt, Esq., Dallas, Texas
Merritt Law Firm
Winner of the Nation Builder award from the
National Black Caucus of State Legislators

Preface

I had a conversation with four of the Five Brothers via telephone before meeting them in person for the first time in February of 2020.

I'm only human and I admit that I had some pre-judgments about what they would be like based on each of our meetings. Some of the interviews were filled with emotion, some were low energy, some were almost manic with very high highs and low lows.

I thought I had developed a sense of which guy was open and generous with his feelings, which one was sensitive and protective of family and friends, which one was affable and charming, which one was super confident with leadership qualities, and which one was vulnerable and loving.

This would be different than any other book project I had taken on because, not only were they five men, they were five successful, intelligent, and handsome young men who were either at the tops of their games professionally and personally, or on their way there.

How will I establish up front that I am as confident as they must be, I wondered the night before the in-person interviews.

Initially, I was going to be joined with media expert and bestie Nikki Woods since the Five Brothers are her clients, but she was on a business trip and stuck somewhere in the Midwest.

I have to have a strategy, I told my husband, David, because if the power shifts too far toward them, I won't be able to get what I need.

"You'll be okay," he said. "Just be yourself."

The site was the Dallas Sheraton, which originally opened 60 years ago.

The downtown jewel was everything Texas (where everything's bigger) claims to be: ostentatious, ambitious, and historic. Once the tallest hotel in the city, in the past it housed the exclusive Chaparral Club Restaurant on the 38th floor that boasted the best view of downtown. The building has been relegated to an "also ran" years ago after it was bested by the taller, newer Renaissance Dallas Hotel, and the famed Chaparral Club is long gone.

Once I got past the covered parking lot, I took an elevator that opened to huge ballrooms, and meeting rooms with that carpet—you know the kind. It reminded me of every other behemoth hotel structure at every other old downtown hotel. Places that were once playgrounds and war rooms for the wealthy and the elite. Places where Ladies Club members lunched and their men smoked cigars and talked about the good old days that were bad old days for everyone but them.

From the ball room area, I would take an escalator. From the top I could see the modernized lobby that mercifully brought me back to the 21st century. As I made my slow decent, I spotted three of the Five Brothers, casual, cool, confident—yes, I got all that from the view above.

Before I reached the bottom, I felt they had spotted me too. We were, as far as I could tell, the only African Americans meeting at 10 a.m. in the lobby of the legendary Dallas Sheraton, a mere block away from the legendary Adolphus Hotel that was once a resting place for KKK members, and three minutes away from the Moorehouse YMCA (now the Dallas Black Dance Theater) which was, until the mid-1960s, one of the few places African Americans passing through Dallas could stay.

And so my heart began to swell with pride the closer I got to the Five Brothers, and something told me that our day together was the beginning of a historic journey.

By the time I reached the area where we would be working, all five were present, and instead of shaking hands, each of them embraced me.

Just like that they were not just *the* Five Brothers, they were *my* Five Brothers: Phillip, Charles, Carlos, Neville, and Travis.

All of my pre-conceived notions immediately disappeared as we sat down and got to work. The adjectives I had tried to label each of them fit all of them. None of them were one thing, none of them from one place, none of them had one experience.

We quickly launched into an icebreaker I made up on the spot. I asked them to describe each other in five words or less.

Their descriptions went as follows:

Phillip/fil-ip
Eager to learn, a listener first, moldable, teachable, a sponge, persistent, relentless, fearless.

Travis/Tra-vis
Taskmaster, analytical, clueless, driven, laid back, understated, an enigma.

Neville/Ne-vil
Random, fun, cocky, disciplined, hustle and flow, critical of the company he keeps.

Carlos/Car-loz
About business, relentless, incomplete, working toward completion and beyond, outspoken, leader, not afraid to make mistakes.

Charles/Charlz
Mellow, cool, suave, suited and booted, iconic, got it goin' on but still chill.

Introduction

Even if they can't recall the exact date, most people old enough to remember can tell you where they were the moment they found out that O.J. Simpson, "The Juice," was on the loose.

On June 17, 1994 for 90 minutes, TV viewers were captivated as the white Ford Bronco driven by O.J. Simpson's ride-or-die, Al Cowlings Jr., crawled down the 405 freeway in Los Angeles.

At the time, one of the world's most recognized and beloved football players turned actor and broadcaster had become a fugitive following a double murder, and was now threatening to take his own life in the most public way possible.

In spite of all of its complexities, the spectacle simply became known as the Bronco Chase and it was one of the most watched TV events in history.

Game 5 of the NBA finals was no competition for this show, nor were any of the things that would have taken us away from network TV today. There were no smart phones, no sophisticated video game systems, and no Netflix streaming original programming back in the 1990s.

Even fans attending the championship game wandered away from their seats to find television monitors in the stadium that were broadcasting the developing story live as police cars trailed behind the slow-moving SUV and news helicopters hovered above.

An estimated 95 million people watched what some called the first reality TV program and pre-curser to the trial of the century. No one knew then that trial would turn attorney Johnnie Cochran into a rock star who would one day have a major impact on the lives of five African-American men, one who was only three years old at the time.

"My mom had just gotten off of a 16-hour work shift at a psych ward in Queens," 29-year-old Phillip Bazemore says.

The subway ride home and subsequent walk to the house, braving the humidity you could count on in Jamaica/Queens New York in June, had already put Carmen in a no-nonsense mood. It didn't help to find Phillip's dad sitting in front of the television.

Like almost every other young man in his early 20s, Thorel had tuned in to watch the New York Knicks take on the Houston Rockets. Instead, he had become mesmerized by the Bronco chase, and oblivious to his young son's situation.

It may not have been the first time Phillip's mom came home and found her toddler in a shitty diaper on his father's watch, but it would be the last.

Phillip says that this was the moment his mother decided it was over between her and Thorel, for good.

On the other side of the country, in Carson, California, a Los Angeles suburb, another father and son were glued to the screen.

Twenty-three-year-old first-year law student Travis Buchanan and his father sat with their mouths open as they witnessed the infamous Bronco Chase together.

"We were watching the playoffs when the news broke and we were like, 'what the heck?'"

At this point, all that was known by most people was that O.J.'s ex-wife Nicole Simpson had been brutally murdered and that the heralded college and NFL legend, O.J. was a suspect.

"I was like, woah, why is he fleeing? I just wanted him to be safe. I didn't want him to get hurt," Travis says.

Down south in Moss Point, Mississippi, 17-year-old Carlos Moore was representing Moss Point High School at Boys State, a national summer leadership program sponsored by the American Legion. Carlos was soon elected governor at the convention, a huge state-wide honor, and a precursor to the political career he would later pursue.

On a farm in Port Antonio, on the northeastern coast of Jamaica, 17-year-old Neville Campbell was preparing to leave his parents and siblings behind to start a brand-new life in the United States. His journey, although filled with obstacles, would eventually include college and medical school.

Being impressionable could have gotten a 20-year-old, smart, ambitious young man like Charles Tucker Jr. into a world of trouble on the streets of Hollis/Queens, New York. But being impressionable actually worked in his favor. Charles had a knack for getting the attention of the right people at the right time and it was already taking him places he'd never imagine being a part of.

Chapter 1: Go Daddy

A father's guiding hand on a son's shoulder will remain with a son forever. —Unknown

A young son of a single mom once quizzically asked his mother, "What do fathers even do?"

It is a heartbreaking commentary about children and the roles their dads should and often do not play in their lives. Depending on which survey you read, between 57 and 72 percent of Black children living in the United States are raised in a household headed by their single mothers. However, the impact fathers or male role models can have on children, whether they're living in the home or not, can be a lasting and positive one.

For the Five Brothers, while very different, each of their dads played monumental roles.

The eldest of four children, raised primarily by his mom, Phillip never held his father's absence against him. Phillip says he was supposed to be Thorel Jr., but his mom tricked his dad and gave him the name of her choice.

"He was who he was," Phillip reasons. Larger than life, his father stood close to 6-foot-5, and his personality earned him a type of status, and even the type of jobs he may have not deserved. Easygoing with accountability issues, Phillip says his dad has a rebellious spirit.

He once saw his father drive down the street, smack into car, and kept driving. His attitude in that situation was the same way it was with a lot of things he did in life: "Welp!"

In spite of that, or maybe because of it, Thorel had a big fan in his son, even when he let Phillip down.

"He did the best he could and he never disappeared."

One Christmas, Phillip recounts, his father came by the house and picked him up.

"I'm thinking we're going shopping at a department store, and I was excited. He took me to the corner store, because that was the best he could do at the time," he says. "But he's also the same guy who rode me to school on the handlebars of my bike. Nobody else's dad was doing that!"

When it comes to most of his family members, especially his father, Phillip's heart is wide open.

"I've always understood him and had high hopes and wants from him, and he's always had the same for me."

On yet another Christmas, like most pre-teens, Phillip wanted to see a video game console under the tree.

"Mom told me flat out, this was not going to be

an Xbox kind of Christmas." But on Christmas day, just like a Super Hero, his dad showed up with one.

"My mom knew he couldn't afford it and she thought that somehow she would be on the hook for it," Phillip says.

She was right.

"My dad had borrowed the money from my uncle and my mom ended up having to pay my uncle back. As bad as it was for her, it did turn out to be an Xbox Christmas after all. Right or wrong, it was my dad who made it happen."

When Carlos was eight years old, his mom, Carolyn, sat him down and explained that the man who raised him, and the only father he had ever known, was not his biological parent.

"I cried for days," he says, and just recounting the story still nearly brings him to tears. Learning the truth that day is not what makes him emotional, though. Instead, it is clearly the love and respect he has for the man who chose to adopt him and raise him as his own, as well as what his mom went through and what she means to him.

There was not a day before or after learning the truth that he was made to feel that he didn't belong.

As he got older, he was able to put the pieces together and process the decisions that his mother made; one that would have huge impacts on both their lives.

"My mom was just 17 when her own mother

died and she went through those challenging teen years without maternal guidance. She was a great student with high potential, and when she became pregnant at age 18, a year after finishing high school, she felt absolutely lost."

Carlos says some people tried to get his mother to have an abortion but she decided against it. She would later meet and marry Anthony Moore, and the three of them became a family, joined later by a sister, Carlissa.

Initially, the shock of finding out that everything he thought he knew about his dad and grandparents was false did have young Carlos doubting his place in his family. He had always spent the summers with his stepdad's side of the family and wondered if the woman he knew as his grandmother, along with the aunts and cousins, could really love him. Of course they did and nothing changed between them.

Still, Carlos' stepdad was upset with Carolyn for telling Carlos the truth. He thought she should have waited a few years until Carlos was older and perhaps could have processed the news differently. But Carlos' mom knew that in a small town like Moss Point, her son needed to know firsthand what so many others already knew about him. As painful as it was hearing it from her, it would have been worse hearing from it someone else.

"I love my dad and never refer to him as my stepfather," he says.

"I eventually met my biological father, Charles

Davis, for lunch when I turned 14, and the next summer he died of cancer. In fairness to him, he told me he would have raised me if given the chance, but he signed for my dad, Anthony, to adopt me because he could see that we were a family," Carlos says.

"My biological father, Charles, had several children and I have had the chance to meet all of my paternal brothers, as well as a paternal sister," he says.

"We have a lot in common and I also discovered similar traits between my father and me, even though we never lived in the same home. I share physical resemblances with him and two of my brothers."

Carlos says he inherited another trait from his biological father, as well.

"My father was also pretty stylish and smooth and so am I. Out of my seven paternal siblings, most of us are married and appear to be intentional about making sure we are raising our children. None of us wanted to pass that job on to another man," he says. That is one of the reasons Carlos is honored to have been adopted by the dad who did raise him.

"My dad taught me to be a man. He taught me by example to have a strong work ethic and morals. He went to work at the shipyards at 6 a.m. and was home every day at 4 p.m."

In spite of an on-the-job injury that caused damage to his back, Carlos says his dad never stopped working. He found employment as a janitor and later a bus driver.

"He only had his GED, but never used not

having a degree as a roadblock to meeting his obligations as a husband and a father. He didn't believe in sitting home and letting a woman take care of him. I knew from watching him that I would always work hard, no matter what."

Travis knew exactly who his father was and his biggest wish as a child was to live with Floyd Buchanan full time. It was his dad's wish, too.

For many years, Travis' dad, a corporate executive at Raytheon, a U.S. defense contractor, fought for full custody of his young son, but the courts thought Travis's mom was better suited for the job.

When Travis was eight years old, his parents divorced, and it was a heavy burden for him and his older sister to bear.

"It was hard especially coming from an upper middle-class community like we did," he says. "I think we were the first family with parents who had separated in our neighborhood. It was a real stigma."

The biggest blow for Travis was the physical separation from his father.

"I really wanted to be with my dad," Travis goes on to say.

"He battled so hard for custody of me, but back then, in the 80s, the mother almost always won custody of the children in divorce cases."

In Travis' and his fathers' minds though, it only made sense for his dad to raise him.

"He was a good man and that's what I needed in

my life."

To make matters worse, Travis' dad made him a promise that, by no fault of his own, he was not able to keep. He assured him that when Travis turned 12, he would be able to decide where he would live full time. His father even made a calendar and he and Travis would mark down the days that would lead to them living together permanently. But when the day finally arrived, they both were devastated by the judge's decision.

"The judge didn't even consider what I wanted," Travis says, still incredulous as to what occurred all of those years ago.

At an early age he got a tough lesson about the court system and how justice could be used against people who were powerless.

Travis discovered that one person was put in charge of making a decision that would have a major impact on his happiness. It would influence the decisions he would make about his own future, but in the meantime, he admits he began to make some bad choices.

Travis' unhappiness drove him to a point of rebellion as he reached his teenage years.

"I started to really get off track, and for the first time my grades began to drop," he recalls.

"I missed a lot of school and wasn't getting the support I needed back then from my mother, even though she continuously fought for custody."

Travis says his dad never gave up on him and

when he'd reached his lowest point academically, his father stepped in and did whatever it took to help him improve his grades.

"If it hadn't been for him, I'm not sure if I would have had the confidence to pursue the career I've chosen."

As Travis made important decisions about college and law school, his father continued to be his biggest supporter, cheerleader and later on, his best friend.

"My father never stopped fighting for me and eventually we won."

Travis lived with his dad in high school and after college while he pursued his law degree.

When Travis got accepted into law school, his father took him to a strip club, an unexpected gesture, yet a real rite of passage in his eyes, he explains.

"It showed me a fun side of my dad as a man that I hadn't seen before. Not only was I surprised that he brought me there, I was surprised that so many of the strippers knew him by name," Travis says with a laugh.

That night, Travis learned that, along with all of the hard work and accomplishments, you have to take time to loosen up and enjoy life, too.

"My dad was very successful. He was a graduate of Pepperdine University's School of Business in Malibu, California and he also received training at the University of Chicago, MIT, and the University of Texas. But he wanted me to see another side to working, traveling, and making money. He also wanted to acknowledge that he saw me as a man and not just his son. Our relationship was turning another corner and he was right by my side as always."

Travis' dad lived to see him graduate from law school and become a skilled prosecutor, however, he passed away from colon cancer April 17, 2004.

The mark he made in Travis's life was indelible. Along with love and examples of how hard work pays off, he had a generous heart too, his son says with pride and emotion. When Travis graduated from law school, his plan was to reward himself with a new Mazda 626, but his dad wanted more for his son.

"You're a lawyer now," he told Travis. "We're going to get you a BMW."

Travis said his father celebrated him, and later Travis had the honor of taking care of his dad during his illness.

"I played tough and would try to stay strong and positive for him. When he died, I couldn't believe he was gone."

In spite of the love he had for his father, Travis says he was not angry at God when he passed away.

"When he was first diagnosed, he had emergency surgery and I prayed for him to make it through. He did, and lived five more years. We made the best of that time together."

Charles had a complicated relationship with his father, Charlie Theodore Tucker Sr., but the love and respect he had for him shined through, even in the dark times.

"The first thing you have to know about my dad is that he was an immigrant from the Bahamas who snuck into the United States at age 16," Charles begins. His telling of the story is a testament to his father's perseverance and also his authoritative nature.

"He was caught, sent back, later returned to the U.S., and then joined the Navy during World War II. Therefore, my four sisters and I grew up in a very militaristic household."

Charles describes that upbringing as strict and with very little room for error.

"We weren't able to leave our rooms until our beds were made, and we had to properly greet our parents first thing each morning," he remembers.

"At meal times we were allowed to take all the food we wanted, but we had to eat all that we took, just like in the Navy."

Charles' dad came to the U.S. with a single goal of building a successful life. He was able to accomplish that despite being a Black immigrant in the 1940s, not the best time for Negroes in America. His drive and ability to serve in the military and gain access to the American dream shaped how he would raise the family he cherished so deeply.

"In his eyes, the seven of us were all we needed," Charles says. "Aside from school and church, my four sisters and I had very little interaction with other children. We were not allowed to hang out on the block or at the homes of other kids in our neighborhood. My dad built a fence around our home, and anyone who wanted to play with us had to be invited in."

It was important to his parents that the family operated as a unit. They strategically created an environment that made them feel that they weren't missing anything that was going on outside of their home.

Along with an expectation of what he wanted from America, he had an expectation of what he wanted from and for his children.

"When we fell short, he had no problem wearing our behinds out. And if one of us did something to warrant a whipping, we all got one."

Utilizing his survival instincts, Charles developed a system to buffer the inevitable physical punishment he would endure.

"I was smart enough to wear an extra pair of pants to ease the pain and, eventually, my sisters caught on and did the same. They took it too far though, sometimes padding themselves with three and four layers of clothing. Of course my father caught on and it ruined it for all of us."

While Charles Tucker Sr. was very adept at showing his family his commitment and dedication toward making sure they succeeded in school and life, he was less skilled at demonstrative and verbal affection.

"I would have liked to have known how my father felt about me and I tried for much of my life to do things that would impress him and make him proud," Charles reflects, clearly overtaken with emotion.

"It wasn't until I was an adult that he told me he loved me. It made me so happy, but I needed to hear those words as a boy."

But as Charlie Tucker Sr. got older, he mellowed out some and his love began to flow freer, especially toward his children and grandchildren, Charles Tucker III in particular. It did him good to see his namesake, Charles says, even though his son was very young when his grandfather, Charlie Sr., died, there was a significance to him celebrating his first birthday with the patriarch of the Tucker family.

"I remember him holding my son in his arms, and, after a while, someone making the motion to take the baby from him to give him a break. My dad was not having it. 'He's fine where he is,' he said."

He passed away three weeks later, and it was almost as though he was determined to bond with his grandson for the last time.

Charles III won't remember those precious moments with his grandfather and it is up to Charles Jr. to let him know the kind of man he was.

Charles is grateful for that opportunity, and he will do it with full appreciation of who is father was and what he has meant to their family.

Looking back, Charles can see contributions that

were missed growing up. If only we all had the advantage of understanding that most parents are doing the best they can with no experience, how much more grace would we have distributed toward them?

Now, as a man and a father himself, Charles knows what it takes to raise a family and keep it together. It takes more than money and things. It takes a commitment and a will to see it through to the end. And it isn't easy. Now, he can relate to being in charge of the lives of Black daughters and a Black son in a country that doesn't value them as much as it should, and probably never will. When Charles looks at what his immigrant father was able to accomplish, he bursts with pride and gratitude.

As an added bonus, Charles' father. had a surprisingly nice amount of savings stored away when he died that Charles' mom and their five adult children were able to benefit from.

"When you're a kid, you spend a lot of time thinking of what your parents did wrong and what you would do differently. But really, there's so much that they did right, and it's up to us to learn from that," Charles says. "My dad was looking out for us even after he was gone."

Charles can only imagine the sacrifices his father made to make that happen.

"That inheritance goes beyond money," he realizes.

It was the kind of provision, protection, and partnership in the future of his family that Charles can only marvel at.

"I wish I could thank him, but I'm sure he knows what it means to us all."

There was one encounter between Neville and his father that changed their relationship for good. He begins with the memories that led up to that day.

"Dad was the enforcer of rules and laws," he says of his Jamaican father, whose name he shares. "We got whippings for everything."

The "we" he refers to includes him and his brother, two years his senior.

"Dad was a perfectionist and if we, for example, didn't properly iron our clothes for school, he would see us on the street and embarrass us in front of our friends. Not only did we have to deal with the embarrassment, we had to go back home and iron our clothes," he says.

Neville says their yard, made up mostly of rocks, dirt, and grass, would be inspected so closely that once, when a candy wrapper was found on the ground, his father took him and his brother to task.

"We had to pick up the wrapper together, each holding one end of it, and carry it a quarter of a mile to the place where the trash was burned."

Neville says the worst part of the story is that neither he nor his brother were responsible for littering. Friends who were gathered at the house to play were asked by his father if they had dropped the wrapper and since they all denied it, Neville and his brother took the heat. After they returned from disposing of the wrapper, they both got several slaps, he says.

"He always had to do the most," Neville remembers; "the most" meaning overdoing any situation that could have been resolved with less severe tactics.

To drive the point home, Neville says the family had cows, chicken, goats, and pigs, and after completing housework, he and his brother would have 12 to 15 pens to wash out.

"Our father thought the pigpens had to be so clean that he should be able to eat his breakfast inside of them without smelling a whiff of the animals. If we failed the test, we would be punished physically."

Most of the whippings were with leather straps that were kept in a particular spot in their home.

"I remember having to go get the strap when Dad was about to discipline us," he says. "We would come back with it and deal with the consequences."

Neville dealt with those consequences for as long as he could. Then, when he was 16 years old, he had enough.

"So you think you're grown now?" Neville's dad asked him repeatedly one day.

Neville says he didn't have an answer to the question, so his dad slapped him down to the ground, twice.

"The third time he asked the question, I got so angry that I bent down and picked up a half of a brick and raised it. My intention was to hit my father upside his head, and I'm sure that the force of the blow would have killed him if I had."

Thankfully, says Neville, his brother slapped the brick out of his hand just in time.

Neville is still grateful to this day that his brother stopped him and he says he is afraid to think of how differently his life would have been if he had been allowed to go through with his action to strike his father at such close range.

Still, the son does not regret the message the gesture of defiance sent to his father.

"When he realized I was going to hit him, he backed off and walked away. He never attempted to put his hands on me again," Neville says.

However, there were lasting repercussions. Neville's father became very distant toward him and that would go on for many years.

"Up until the time I left for the States at age 18, we barely spoke to each other."

Even when Neville was planning to marry, his father was wary about attending his youngest son's wedding. Eventually, Neville's sisters persuaded their father to go, but even still their relationship was strained.

Neville was a grown man and it was difficult for his dad to realize that he could not be intimidated any longer. In fact, most of his siblings have gotten past those feelings of fear their father once elicited.

As time went on, Neville's father grew to accept

the fact that his son was an adult and had his own ideas about doing things.

"When he visits and makes recommendations about the way something is being done around the house, I can tell him I am comfortable the way it is. That wasn't easy for him to grasp at first."

Neville believes that his father's very difficult childhood played a big role in the aggression he showed toward almost everyone, including Neville's mother. As a young child, the senior Neville was already working to take care of his own ill mother and younger sisters. In most cases he was the youngest person on the jobs he held and undoubtedly had to stand up to employers and co-workers.

His father never had a real childhood because he had so many responsibilities as a little boy, Neville says. "He was thrust into manhood at a very early age. He had to learn to read and write on his own and still was able to find success as a man, a husband, and a father," Neville explains with a bit of compassion.

"As he provided for his family, he had very little patience with anyone who had an excuse for not accomplishing the goals he had set for us. To him, nothing we attempted was too difficult and we should have found a way to get it done."

Compared to his father's childhood, Neville and his siblings had it easy, and that may be why he made sure they were going beyond what was expected of most children their ages.

Neville remembers having a huge tree in his yard

that shed lots of foliage. His father demanded that the ground remained pristine, so he and his brother were constantly picking up leaves.

"If we didn't pay attention to every detail when we were cleaning the yard, the pigpens or the inside of our house, our dad would call us nasty and dirty," he explains, his emotions going from empathy to frustration.

Neville admits that living under those kinds of conditions for so many years led to him developing obsessive compulsive tendencies.

"At one point in my life, everything had to be perfect in my home, nothing could be out of place."

Once he began to understand why he was this way, he worked to get better and has learned to get past much of that behavior. He has also worked to heal the relationship he has with his father.

"I returned to Jamaica three years ago and said, man, let's put this to rest. We are both men and there is never any need for you to yell or speak to me in the tone that you did when I was a child."

Neville established much needed boundaries in their relationship, and he is pleased with the outcome.

"We still are not what you would consider as tight, but there is a level of mutual respect now," Neville contends.

"My dad proudly tells his friends and family that he has a son in the states who is a doctor. He doesn't tell me he is proud of me," he says with a smile. "But I know he is."

Chapter 2: Mama's Boys

Listen, my son, to your father's instruction and do not forsake your mother's teaching. They are a garland to grace your head and a chain to adorn your neck. –Proverbs 1:8-9

The Five Brothers' families come in all sizes and genders.

Travis has two half sisters, and one half-brother, Neville has five brothers and two sisters, Carlos grew up with one sister but has half brothers and a half sister he met later in life, Charles has four sisters and no brothers, and Phillip has one younger brother and two younger sisters. And while their fathers were all major forces in their lives, their mothers were equally impactful and, in some cases, their relationships with their moms just as complex.

Embroiled in the middle of a bitter custody battle for much of his childhood, at one time, Travis was certain that he would practice family law.

"My mom fought to keep me, even though she didn't want me, just to get back at my dad," he says with more regret in his voice than anger.

Travis says because of his strained relationship with his mother, he often depended on his older sister for support. "She's always been there for me," he says.

Even though Travis says he's moved past the pain brought on by his mom keeping him from living with his father, it is hard to believe that the wounds have healed completely. It is more like they have been covered with a flesh-colored band aid that is barely noticeable until ripped off. Others may not be aware of it, but the sting is still there.

Travis and his sister now both live in Las Vegas, and when their mom visits from California for the holidays, Travis says she comes to his home for dinner but never has spent the night there.

"She stays at my sister's house," he says and adds that he's never actually asked her to spend more time at his home. "Maybe it's to protect myself," he reasons.

Travis does acknowledge that the unfinished business between him and his mother has had an impact on his own family.

"Now that my daughters are older, they ask me questions about my relationship with my mother and I've told them about some of the things that happened to me growing up."

Still, Travis and his mother have yet to re-hash the events of the past. And he seems content to leave it there. He considers what he went through as a life lesson of sorts.

"Mom takes credit for my accomplishments now. I will give her credit for motivating me to be a better person and to treat people the way I want to be treated," he says.

Travis has plenty of compassion for parents, especially fathers' battles for the rights to gain custody of their children. For this reason, he says, he was certain once that he would practice family law. But to his surprise, he discovered that tackling those kinds of cases were too emotionally taxing for him.

"After taking on one family law case, I quickly saw that I hated it," he recalls. "It was too negative, and there was too much fighting over petty things like the family dog," he says. "I didn't like watching adults trying to get at each other. I saw enough of that firsthand."

Instead, Travis became a prosecutor and uses his expertise to help people get large settlements and resolutions, something that brings him plenty of satisfaction.

"I like that. I make clients happy by turning wrongs into rights."

Judge Carlos E. Moore thinks the world of his mom, Carolyn, and the fact that she made the decision to have him in spite of the odds she faced makes his relationship with her even more special.

"Mom cried the whole day I was born," he says, retelling the story that has been relayed to him. Even facing the hardships of going through her teenage years without her mother, Carlos' mom did very well in high school.

"She was a go-getter, and no one expected her to get pregnant so soon after graduating," he says.

"But, while visiting her sister in California, she met my father, Charles Davis, who was originally from our hometown of Moss Point and landed there after being in the military."

Carlos says, from the start, his mother was facing a challenge of single motherhood but she never gave up.

"Once I got here, she didn't know how she was going to raise me," he says.

But she quickly figured it out, going about her new life as a mother with the same persistence and passion she had as a student. After marrying the man who would become Carlos' dad, Anthony Moore, the two did everything they could to help Carlos, and later his younger sister, become successful. While his dad worked double shifts and sometimes held two or three jobs at a time, it was his mom who was present at every event, pushing Carlos and supporting him along the way, despite the fact that she also worked.

"She always made a way to take off to attend school and church events that we took part in," Carlos says.

"The faith she had in me was a confidence booster throughout my life."

Carlos also recalls how his mom would take him

to the library when he was a junior in high school to research which scholarships were available and she continued to help her only son in any way she could throughout high school, college, law school, and beyond.

Carolyn's commitment toward seeing Carlos meet his goals included spiritual, emotional, and financial support.

Right out of law school, Carlos was hired by a firm and doing well, so well that he asked his boss for a raise. When he was refused the raise he felt he deserved, Carlos decided to set out on his own and planned to open his own law firm. He had everything necessary to make the move except the money. Knowing what having his own firm would mean to him, his mother stepped out on faith.

"She gave me the $35,000 I needed to fulfill my dream," he says, choking back tears.

To some, it would be considered a gamble for Carlos' mom to use her retirement money for her son's firm, a gamble that she couldn't afford to take.

But Carolyn looked at it more as an investment in a future that she had no doubt would be abundantly fruitful.

It turned out that her investment was a smart one. After three years of practicing law, Carlos paid his mom back in full.

"She raised my sister and me to believe we could be anything we wanted to be and she was always there for us. I never wanted to let her down," Carlos says.

"I am eternally grateful to her for always believing in me," he says.

When Attorney Charles Tucker Jr.'s parents decided to try to have another son to balance out the family that included two older sisters and Charles, they had twin girls instead.

Always outnumbered by women in his home, Charles settled in with that truth and rarely tried to fight it. He was right in the middle and because of it, he says, he could jump double dutch with the best of the girls.

"My sisters say I'm a Mama's Boy, but I have never felt that way," he says.

Charles has great love for his mom, but never felt that she spoiled him in any way. If anything, he felt that his sisters were always a priority and he was frequently the recipient of their leftovers.

Since Charles' mother emigrated from her home country after marrying his father, she had very little family in the United States.

"We never were surrounded by a lot of aunts, uncles, and cousins, like families who have been here for two and three generations," Charles says.

Because of this, his mother put most of her focus on her children, and especially her daughters.

In a way, though, she herself grew up in the United States, too, having married his dad when she was just 19 years old. His father was 44.

In fact, Charles' mother's own father, who was

the Prime Minister of Nicaragua at the time, was four years younger than Charles' dad.

"Needless to say, my grandfather was not happy about this union for two reasons, first because of the age difference and, second, because my father was Black."

But love won out and Charlie Tucker and his young bride moved into their home in Hollis/Queens in 1965. The two would maneuver through life in their new country together.

While they may have argued about a lot of things, Charles says they were solid and remained committed to their marriage and to their children.

There was no doubt that they loved each other in spite of their reluctance to demonstrate it publicly or in front of their own children, for that matter.

"My parents were not overly affectionate toward each other, but my mom commanded respect from my father and I almost never saw him cross the line."

Charles says there was rarely any cursing or ugly language used by either of his parents nor was there any drinking.

"If my father started to bring some bad language into the house, my mom would threaten to take a rolling pin to his head."

Charles' mom knew that her husband liked the horses and accepted his gambling habit, even though she did not encourage it, he says.

"If my dad came home late from work, it was because one of his horses won a race. He would have extra food and would come in counting his money. She trusted him."

Charles says there was no escaping his mother's Central American roots or the looks received when the two of them were together, mother and son. She is a light-skinned Hispanic woman who could pass for white, and Charles is darker-skinned like his dad.

"I'd be walking with my mom and people would be looking at me like, who dat," he says with a laugh.

Charles says if he was special to either of his parents for being the only son, neither of them let him know it or feel it. They worked very hard to provide everything they needed and, in their minds, that was enough to make it in this country that they were blessed to have been born in.

"I would have liked to have had more positive reinforcement from either of them," Charles says. "I needed it."

Phillip Bazemore's mom, Carmen, is a hard-working, light-hearted woman with a great personality. But as Phillip was growing up, she always seemed to be in an uphill battle, he says, most likely because of the pressure she applied on herself.

"She required greatness," Phillip says.

Phillip says his mom leaned heavily on him to partner with her in caring for his younger siblings, primarily his brother who was four years his junior. Phillip, even at a young age, did not take that responsibility lightly.

Since Carmen was a single mom until Phillip turned eleven, Phillip was taught to fill in for her while she worked.

Aside from making certain his brother and sisters were out of harm's or mischief's way, his job was also to do well in school so that he would be prepared for the bright future his mother was sure he would have.

"My mom had high expectations of me and supported me the best way she knew how. She wanted me to be either a doctor or a lawyer, but her desires came with no roadmap," Phillip says.

"So much more than what my mother was able to give was required for a kid like me to make it out of the neighborhood I grew up in," he explains.

In Jamaica/Queens, just getting home safely from school every day was a challenge.

"I had to be responsible for me as well as my little brother. I didn't get a chance to get into too much mischief because, if I took five steps, he would take fifteen. I always had to be conscious of where he was because I didn't want him to get into trouble."

Phillip and his mom also shared in a partnership in success, as well, that began when Carmen was a student attending community college, and would bring him to class with her each day.

"I would sit in the back of the class doing busy work while she worked toward her goal."

Phillip says his mom was careful not to leave him in unsafe environments, so he would frequently accompany her when she hung out with her friends.

"We became close out of necessity," he says. "I did things with her that most boys weren't doing with their moms, and, eventually, it became a friendship type of thing."

Even though Carmen wasn't the kind of mom who involved her children in her decisions, Phillip remembers that she made a point of getting his opinion on Warren, the man who would become his stepfather, before things moved to a more serious level.

"I was okay with it. I wanted my mom to be happy and Warren made her completely happy."

As difficult as it sometimes was for his mom financially, Phillip says Carmen was always trying to get him the things she believed he deserved out of life, including a good education. She wanted the same for herself, as well, as she strived toward getting a bachelor's degree before her son, something she did accomplish, Phillip says with pride.

She also made sacrifices for Phillip that he wasn't always able to appreciate.

"When I was in high school, my mom paid for me to go on a bus tour to Black colleges. It was an amazing experience, and because of it, I had my heart set on going to Hampton University or Howard. But when it was time to apply for colleges, she told me I couldn't go to school out of state because it was too expensive. That was devastating to me. Why even send me on the tour?" he wondered.

Even with these types of disappointments, Phillip says his mom was the only one telling him something positive and setting standards, disciplining him and providing for him.

There was a time when believed that his mom fell short when it came to fulfilling her end of the bargain. As a 22-year-old, he thought that she could have done more to help him live up to her expectations. But looking back, he recognizes that he was going through an "everyone is against me" phase.

Phillip says even though he took to heart the things his mother said to him about becoming a doctor or a lawyer, as an adult, he now understands how limited her own knowledge was about what that would actually take.

"So much of what she said was just to help keep me on track."

"My mom would tell me what she wanted from me and I would do it. I did everything I could to live up to her expectations and I felt like a failure whenever I fell short, even though I may have been doing much better than a lot of the guys I grew up with."

Even still, Phillip believes he caused his mom a lot of problems.

"I would do things like get a bead stuck up my nose and my mom would have to leave work and come to school to check on me," he says.

His mom had big dreams of her own, Phillip says, noting that she is both smart and beautiful.

"She was a runner-up in the Miss Connecticut beauty contest and a psychology major in college. But she had me at age 21 and had the added responsibility of taking care of her ill parents," he says. "With all of her aspirations, I know she had no intentions of having a child so young."

Like fans at a marathon yelling "keep going" with no inkling of the pain and fatigue the runners are feeling, or the grueling training they endured to prepare for the race, Phillip's mom continued to cheer him on.

"She planted the seed for me to become an attorney, and I'll always be grateful for that."

When Phillip got accepted into law school, it was a very proud moment for Carmen, but due to an unfortunate event, Phillip had to leave law school and he says that news devastated his mom.

When he got back in school, for him it was an even bigger accomplishment, but Phillip says his mom didn't share his enthusiasm the second time around. He needed to prove to her that he could succeed this time. She no longer seemed to have the blind faith in him that she once did.

Like his mom taught him by example, Phillip pushed through and accomplished the goal of graduating from law school.

"My mom's persistence is something I'm very proud of," Phillip says.

Carmen fearlessly went after the things she wanted in life.

In the mid-2000s, real estate prices had begun to peak and right before the bubble when prices sank to record lows, Phillip's mom bought some property in Ohio with the intention of flipping it and making a large profit.

"It didn't go well," Phillip says, "but I was so proud of her for trying. Whether it's improving herself through education or losing 40 pounds, she continues to invest in herself and her family, no matter what.

"Overall, she's never disappointed me."

He hopes she'd say the same about him.

"A vast majority of goodness in me comes from Mom," Dr. Neville Campbell says.

His mother, Esmine, grew up with a more traditional family structure than his father did, with lots of sisters and two nurturing parents.

Much of the story Neville tells about his mom revolves around the meeting between her and his father. It begins when Neville's mom was a young woman living in Jamaica's St. Elizabeth Parish with her husband whom he calls Mr. Gayle, and their three children.

Despite the fact that St. Elizabeth Parish was known as a producer of sugar and many prospered from the fishing industry, Esmine found it difficult to find work. When her older sister invited her to come to Port Antonio where there were more opportunities for employment, Esmine agreed to work alongside her in a grocery shop.

Even though Neville's mom missed her family, she was able to see the benefits of working steadily and contributing to the family back in St. Elizabeth.

Esmine frequently wrote to Mr. Gayle but because her sister wanted her to remain in Port Antonio, she and her husband Mr. Brooks played a cruel hoax by never mailing the letters! After going so long without hearing from his Esmine, Mr. Gayle understandably decided to move on.

Esmine was heartbroken to learn that Mr. Gayle had given up on their relationship, but the reality was that the relationship was sabotaged by Esmine's sister and her husband. They believed that Mr. Gayle was not the right man for Esmine. He was a nice, hard-working gentleman, but he was much older than Esmine, and that did not sit well with her family.

Once it was clear that Esmine was no longer attached to Mr. Gayle, her sister lined up some businessmen of means for her to meet. But once fate brought Neville, whom Neville was named for, her way, the other potential suitors were out of luck.

Even though the senior Neville already had fathered two children in a previous relationship, he and Neville's mom began to date.

Neville Sr. was not as financially stable as some of the men Esmine had been introduced to, but there was something she saw in him.

The two married and moved into Neville Sr.'s one-room home with the five children they had between the two of them.

Young Neville and his brother were born nearly 10 years after the sister who was the youngest of the original bunch. By this time, Neville's father had added multiple rooms to the house and also indoor plumbing. Neville's father had also become an entrepreneur with numerous employees helping him run the farm.

While the senior Neville served as provider, young Neville's mother took care of the home. She made sure they were doing their homework even though, Neville notes, she herself had never completed grade school.

"Mom is a kind soul, almost to the detriment of her own health and sanity," Neville says.

"She always shared whatever we had with strangers passing by our home."

Neville says his mom's generosity would be upsetting to his father and sometimes to him and his siblings, as well. Even if there was not enough for the family to eat, if someone was in need, that would not stop her from sharing what they had.

"To this day, people will come over to our family home and tell her they remember what she did for them," Neville says.

And her contributions went well beyond food.

"They remind her of how she showed them respect and compassion when they had nothing."

Along with being a caretaker and problem solver for others, she was all that and more for his family, including a peacemaker, in spite of all of the drama his father brought their way.

In fact, it was her love that may have saved Neville's father's life.

"Dad has gotten into so many verbal altercations with people on our road over the years, men have actually told me and my brother that if it had not been for my mom, they would have killed him," Neville says.

"We can't even say, 'What are you talking about?' because we know."

That's the kind of power Neville's mom, Esmine, had that she is still spreading to those she meets.

That is the power of kindness and love.

Chapter 3: Excellence

Who is this freaking Negro?
–Charles Tucker Jr.

If the Five Brothers—four attorneys and a physician—have a single commonality, it is the standard of excellence they have set for themselves, and they are each passionate about it in their own way.

Charles and Carlos, who became law partners not long after meeting in 2016, formed a bond that would open the door for other young Black lawyers who were interested in creating a network that celebrated excellence. Charles describes the pair as the City Slicker and the Country Boy.

"I'm from New York and he's from Mississippi. But we both had so much in common aside from wanting to mentor young lawyers. I'm older but he became the big brother because, well, he's Carlos. He's a leader and he goes after what he wants. I'm the good cop, he's the bad cop, but I always have his back."

Carlos and Charles had joined The Cochran Firm, founded by the late Johnnie L. Cochran, and recruited another young gun, Travis, who was headquartered in Las Vegas. The group of young men became a force when the three of them were at a trial lawyer's event in Miami, Florida with the plan to meet a doctor who Travis had hoped to bring into the fold.

Carlos, Travis, and Charles had rented a condo on Miami Beach and Charles describes their first encounter with Neville.

"Campbell walks in with a Louis Vuitton luggage bag and other matching accessories and I thought to myself, who is this freaking Negro," he recounts with a big laugh. "He took over the whole event."

Neville was clearly on a mission and that was to establish himself as the most successful, high-profile physician in Las Vegas, and he knew he needed connections from all over to make that happen.

"I took my family from New York to Las Vegas on a whim," Neville explains.

"I was starting a new business with no support but I knew I was great at building connections. Either I would be calling them or they would be calling me," he says of the people he would meet.

"In order to make it work, I had to be that guy. I needed to know the key players in Las Vegas and to let them know why they should shift from the doctors they already had and begin a relationship with me."

When Neville met Travis, they both discovered that they needed to become a force in Vegas' community by meeting with all of the relevant businesses there.

"I was impressed to see other Black professionals in the medical and legal arena, and I decided to make it my duty to connect us all. We joined forces by sharing clients," he said.

"Travis and I decided that when either of us had opportunities or cases, we would send them to each other. That business relationship turned into friendship," he says.

But it goes beyond that, the Five Brothers agree. Because they are certain that God has a hand in it, they have vowed that everything they do will be done with excellence and in order. It is upsetting to them when it appears that some clients have grown accustomed to getting less than that.

"People walk into our offices expecting public squalor," Neville says. "Why? I want to re-write the misconception they have in their minds. Don't expect that I will act or speak a certain way because I am Black."

He says that what he and the Brothers are trying to do for their communities is a combination of hustle, flow and divine intervention.

Charles adds that it is imperative that Black people help each other to continue to raise the bar for what they expect from each other on a professional level.

"Black excellence is not the norm yet, let's be real. It can be but it isn't yet," he says.

"Too often Black professionals have great

achievements and move on, never giving back to the communities they've left behind," Charles says.

The Brothers are determined to offer to others what they wish had been offered to them when they were striving to reach their professional goals.

Enter Phillip, the youngest of the crew. He is the product of their collective mentoring.

"Phillip latched on to us at a mixer and immediately started soaking in everything he heard from us. And he also shared a lot about himself. He would start talking, giving us bits and pieces that had nothing to do with nothing," Charles says jokingly.

"We learned in a short amount of time about where he grew up, some of the challenges he was experiencing, and what he needed. We knew that between the four of us, there was something we could do to help him."

The Brothers used their connections and became a support system for Phillip.

Phillip says what he has learned from the Brothers has been immeasurable. They have embraced him in a way that few men have and he feels honored to be included in what they have created. He considers them all to be his mentors and will continue to soak up the knowledge they impart.

Phillip adds that there will be many more young attorneys who will be helped by the Brothers and that is fine with him.

"I'm not the last piece, I'm the latest," he says.

Charles says what the Brothers are doing with

young men like Phillip makes their goal of continuing a legacy of Black excellence crucial.

But, is there a difference between excellence and Black excellence? Charles says emphatically that there is.

"Excellence is performing at the highest level. Black excellence is an understanding that there is an obligation to make sure that others reach that level of performance as well.

Chapter 4: Independence Day

A man will show his true colors in adversity.
−African Proverb

"I'm a law student, I'm not resisting!" These are the words Phillip repeated as he was being beaten and kicked by four white police officers on July 4, 2011.

The evening began innocently enough. His younger brother Todd was visiting him in Jacksonville, Florida and they had decided to check out fireworks near the beach. A cousin was going to be there, too, so they anticipated a fun evening ahead.

The area was packed with people in the street. It was a scene we've all witnessed on one Fourth of July or another. Music, laughter, running, dancing, and yelling just to be able hear yourself talk over it all. It was a carefree holiday night heightened by crowds and pending excitement of a show that promised to light up the sky. Nothing is more American than that.

Phillip was on the phone with the cousin he and his brother were planning to meet up with when a police officer made eye contact with him and said, "Get the fuck on the sidewalk."

The officer followed the command by asking, "What did you say to me?"

"I was on the phone and hadn't said anything to him," Phillip says.

"The next words out of his mouth were 'Get the fuck over here.'"

Phillip admits that his next move was an immature one but he was a 22-year-old kid at the time.

"It was like when you know your parents are calling you, but you act like you don't hear them," he says, feeling the need to explain his action.

"I was far enough away from the officer that I thought he would think I didn't hear him."

Phillip's brother was in front of him. Phillip caught up to him and told him to keep walking. While taking steps away from the voice of the irate officer, suddenly the one who had spoken so harshly to him ran ahead and jumped on his brother's back.

"My brother is huge. He was just 18 but six-foot-four, the size of our father."

That officer put Todd in a choke hold, Phillip says, and before Phillip knew it, another officer grabbed his right arm and right hooked him in the face, barroom style.

"I didn't fight back. The only thing I had done was look him in the eyes and say, 'that was such a pussy move,' as I voluntarily got on my knees with my hands behind my back."

Unfortunately for Phillip, that was only the beginning. While Phillip was on his knees, the officer kicked him in the back of the head.

"Stop resisting," the officer yelled.

Phillip knew that meant he was about to get his ass kicked, and that is exactly what happened.

Afterwards, while down on the ground, Phillip was Tased three times and laid in the fetal position and then was cuffed, facing sideways on the street.

Before escorting Phillip to the police car, the cop made one final statement as a crowd looked on in disbelief.

"He grinds my face into the cement."

All in one night, Phillip's life was about to take a detour. He had gotten through college and grad school and was set to enter law school.

"I went to a program called Ample and if you had a B-plus average, you would get accepted into Florida Coastal Law School, sort of a last chance institution," he explains. Phillip says he didn't have the best grades in graduate school, but was prepared to pay the price by finishing the Ample program and heading to a law school with others who for one reason or another were in the same boat as he was.

The final exam was scheduled for right after the July Fourth holiday.

Before getting into the police car, Phillip used his cell phone to call his grandmother. He told her he was going to jail. He didn't know which jail or which precinct.

It was 1 a.m. and he had just been beaten bloody. The officer responsible for the act of brutality grabbed his phone and slammed it to the ground, shattering it into a thousand pieces, Phillip says.

"My brother was down and I yelled to him not to get up. 'Don't move,' I told him."

Even in the worst situation of his life, Phillip remembered that his brother was first and foremost his responsibility. "I'm so thankful that he listened to me."

They both went to jail that morning. At the police station, while in his cell, Phillip had his first encounter with a Black officer.

"What are you doing hitting cops," he asked. "Who did I hit?" Phillip says he yelled.

The officer who beat him walked up to his cell, laughing. "You hit me, him, him, and him," he said pointing to various officers.

That morning Phillip was thrown around in the cell and had his head slammed against the wall, all while in chains.

Later they sent Phillip to a containment facility where he was lucky enough to get a cot.

"Only the strong survive. I wasn't the strongest but I wasn't the weakest, either."

Phillip says he traded his food for a phone call and called his mom. She told him she would try to figure something out.

"It wasn't fun. People were getting their food and beds taken, and the recreational activities included guys playing dice, and doing pull-ups under the steps."

The day Phillip got out of jail was the day he would take his final exam that would determine whether he would be fortunate enough to be headed to "Last Chance" law school.

"I showed up for class with my face torn apart, battered, and bruised," he says. "But, none of us taking the exam had many options."

The following day the results came out. Phillip had passed.

"Nothing else mattered. While I was taking the test, I was locked in. I only thought about the material. It was beautiful and I really thought everything that happened that night at the beach was behind me."

But it was not behind him. Not by a long shot.

"I was charged with violently resisting arrest, which is a felony. They dropped the battery to officer charges, but the violently resisting arrest charges they wouldn't drop," he says.

With neither his mom or stepfather knowing much about legal representation, and Phillip being miles away in Florida, his dad took a leading role and hired an average to less-than-average attorney.

"I was advised that I couldn't beat the case. This was a frustrating introduction into law," Phillip says.

"After a review of my background, the judge allowed me to do community service, write letters of apology, and have an adjudication upheld on the felony charge. Since my brother was under age, he went to juvenile court and his case was dismissed."

Phillip says it was challenging going to court and

law school at the same time, and by the end of the semester his grade point average was 2.7.

Midterms were coming the same week his probation officer told him he wasn't doing a good job completing his community service hours.

"She told me I would have to do all 50 hours that week or go to AA," Phillip says.

"I went to AA every day instead of studying and bottomed out. It was horrible. I was academically dismissed and eventually kicked out of law school. It crushed my mom. She was the first person out of all of her friends who had a kid in law school."

Life for Phillip sank even lower. He left Florida and moved to New York, which was one of the worst places in the world to be broke. He says he moved into a disgusting apartment with a co-worker from at a catering job he had gotten. When his mom came to see him for Thanksgiving, he wouldn't even allow her to see the way he was living.

But the sun rose again.

Phillip heard that Last Chance law school was struggling and that he should reapply. He did, and was accepted. More than two years had passed since he was asked to leave.

"Most of the students didn't even know I had been kicked out," Phillip says.

This time around, without all of the stress, he was starting to do well in school.

"I missed one question on my contracts exam and got an A instead of an A-plus," he says.

But the story does not end here, and even though Phillip has repeated it several times in life, you can feel his pain as he relives that harrowing night in Florida. It is an encounter that put his life into a tailspin and he is yet to recover completely.

Chapter 5: South Mississippi Strong

Our lives begin to end the day we become silent about things that matter.
–Dr. Martin Luther King Jr.

When Carlos was a little boy, he and his family enjoyed watching TV show reruns that featured attorneys like "Perry Mason" and the hit series "L.A. Law."

"I wanted to become a lawyer even back then, but my parents were against it because they said lawyers had to lie."

Carlos decided to become a doctor instead, and there was no reason to believe his dream would not come to fruition. He was fiercely competitive and second place was never good enough. He recounts a story about setting out to become valedictorian of his kindergarten class.

"I was mad when I ended up being salutatorian," he says. "But I did become valedictorian in the 6th grade."

He later became the student body president at Moss Point High School and Salutatorian of his senior class. From there, he attended the University of South Alabama in Mobile where he served as President of the Black Student Union for two years.

Carlos entered college as a pre-med student and all was going as planned until he missed the guaranteed spot for medical school.

"I felt like I was a failure," Carlos says.

But deep down inside he knew better. He was used to accomplishing everything he'd attempted, so it didn't take him long to set his sights on something he'd wanted deep down since he was a child. He changed his major to political science and decided to become a lawyer after all. After obtaining a political science degree in 1999, Carlos attended Florida State University College of Law where earned a Juris Doctorate in 2002.

Carlos has gone on to rack up an impressive list of honors such as Outstanding Young Lawyer of Mississippi by the Mississippi Bar in 2008, the first African American to ever receive the prestigious award. Most recently, in May of 2020, Carlos was named the first ever African-American Municipal Court Judge Pro Tem in Grenada, Mississippi, where he resides. Then, in the summer of 2020, Carlos was elected president of the National Bar Association, the nation's oldest network of predominately Black lawyers and judges.

Carlos got his first Civil Rights case in 2006. Realizing that he didn't have the expertise needed, he hired a more experienced lawyer who happened to be white. Together, they succeeded and Carlos' firm went on to represent many more clients in Civil Rights cases.

One of his biggest battles has been against the Mississippi State Flag that includes the Confederate emblem.

As a kindergarten student striving to become first in his class, Carlos saluted that flag because he had no choice. That flag also flew over his alma mater, Moss Point High School, and it flew over the State Capitol building in Jackson, Mississippi in 2020.

On June 17, 2015, white supremacist Dylann Roof gunned down nine African Americans during a Bible Study meeting at Emanuel African Methodist Episcopal Church in Charleston, South Carolina. Despite the fact that heinous racial attack spurred the states of South Carolina and Alabama to cease flying the Confederate Flag above their State Houses, the Mississippi legislature continued to vote against the removal of its state flag.

But, in February, less than a year after the Dylann Roof mass murder, then-governor of Mississippi, Phil Bryant, made an announcement that made Carlos' blood boil.

"He chose Black History Month to say that the state of Mississippi would celebrate Confederate Heritage Month, starting in April."

Carlos decided right then and there to challenge the flag in the federal court system, citing that it was a violation of the Equal Protection Clause.

"I drove from Grenada, Mississippi to Jackson to file the lawsuit the same month," Carlos says.

The 100-plus mile trek was well worth it to Carlos who believed he had the state's racist history to draw from.

The primary reason that Mississippi seceded from the Union was because of its support of slavery and that flag represents the disenfranchisement of Black people, he points out.

And that wasn't all.

Carlos' suit not only had to prove why he believed the flag was a racist symbol but also the damaging impact the flag had on him personally. He had medical documents to back up the fact that seeing the Confederate flag elevated his heart rate and caused his blood pressure to spike.

Governor Bryant attempted to ignore the suit by refusing to respond to Carlos' petition. However, the Supreme Court eventually asked him to respond, which was a banner day for Carlos.

Even though the case was not won, Carlos is certain that he was on the right course.

"All of the Civil Rights advancements in Mississippi have come through the federal court system, including the integration of the University of Mississippi, and the integration of public schools."

Carlos did achieve a personal victory when he took a stance closer to home.

July 10th of 2017 he was appointed the first

African-American Municipal Judge Pro Tem for the
city of Clarksdale, and his first order of business was
to demand that the Mississippi State Flag be removed
from his court room.

"I could not have that flag displayed behind me
as I attempted to administer justice," he says.

"That flag does not stand for justice," he
reiterates.

However, Carlos is clear about what the state
flag of Mississippi does stand for.

"The subjugation of my people, lynchings,
murder, and enslavement," he says.

Carlos has called himself a proud American and
a conflicted Mississippian.

"Mississippi is the last state to fly that flag," he
says.

"We're supposed to honor that flag in spite of
what it stands for? My little daughter is expected to
honor that flag?"

The pledge to the state flag goes as follows:
*I salute the flag of Mississippi and the
sovereign state for which it stands with pride
in her history and achievements and with
confidence in her future under the guidance of
Almighty God.*

"No," says Carlos. "I want to salute a flag that
represents all of the citizens of Mississippi, not one
that represents white supremacists."

Carlos, of course, was not alone in his fight, and in June of 2020, the traditional state flag containing the Confederate emblem was finally retired. A new flag featuring a magnolia, the state's flower, is set to replace it. As of this printing, the New Magnolia is awaiting approval from voters in a November 2020 election.

"I have to believe I played a part in that flag coming down," Carlos says, noting that he won the moral battle. "It's a huge and satisfying victory."

Chapter 6: Angels

Echoes of mercy, whispers of love.
–Frances J. Crosby, "Blessed Assurance"

Dr. Neville Campbell can chronicle multiple times in life where people have seemingly come out of nowhere and saved him from hurt, harm, and even deportation.

"I was so happy to get away from that damn farm when my aunt told me to come to the States," Neville says. "She told me to come there, live with her family, and go to college. But the promises she made were not realized," he says.

Neville says he arrived in the Bronx in August of 1995 ready to enroll in college. "My aunt told me she was working on it. By September, I still wasn't in school and she finally confessed that she didn't have the money for me to go. I cried in her living room."

It was the first September that Neville could remember that he wasn't in school.

"I watched the buses come to take her kids and I was not one of them. I was not mentally prepared for that letdown."

Neville's aunt had misled him. He says she had

no intentions of him going to school and her primary goal was to get help with her house and kids.

"For three months, I did the cooking, the cleaning, and did not go to school," Neville says. A visit from his brother changed everything.

"He thought I was in school and was furious to find out what I was actually doing. He went off on my aunt. When he left, she called me rude and disrespectful."

She also gave Neville notice he had two weeks to find somewhere else to live.

"I left her home and got involved in church. The members knew right away that something was not right. I never told them I was homeless but they knew. They were my first set of angels."

Neville would be invited to his church members' homes and kept moving from place to place.

"They saw that my shoes were worn and I had no jacket. The next week, those things would be provided," he says. "These angels of God provided me with meals and free places to stay. No charge. I was never out in the cold."

Eventually, Neville got hired as a busboy at a New York restaurant, earning $4.75 per hour. He would keep that job for two years.

"I was used to working and, because my father was so meticulous, I paid very close attention to detail," he says.

"I was the best busboy they had ever seen."

Compared to making sure that the pigpens on his

father's farm were spotless and odorless, cleaning tables and washing dishes was nothing.

Even though it was his original plan to finish undergraduate college and enter medical school in a span of about five years, it actually took Neville ten years to get to medical school once he arrived in the U.S., and the road was rough.

In 1997, Neville left the restaurant and started a job at a brokerage/ management company.

"I worked in data entry and learned everything on the job. I had no experience at all. I wasn't qualified when I started but I could not fail."

Neville trained himself to learn Microsoft Excel. In time he got better, and eventually became very proficient. He was so determined and dependable that his co-workers began to root for him, something you wouldn't normally expect from New Yorkers.

Neville was promoted and his manager reminded him that she would need to see proof that he was in the country legally.

"I put her off for as long as I could and years passed. Finally, she stopped asking," Neville says. "She knew I did not have my papers and she could have had me deported, but she didn't."

Another angel.

In 1995, Neville met his wife Tashi, and it was with her encouragement that he began to seriously pursue the education he so desperately wanted in America. The two were married in 1999 and had their first baby girl not long after.

In 2003, Neville began night school and enrolled in State University of New York (SUNY), now known as Purchase College, and finished four years of college in two years, including summers.

"I had no money," Neville admits. "I had to put all of my time and energy into finishing college. My wife worked hard and cared for our little girl."

His next feat after graduating from college would be medical school, and God opened that door for him too, says Neville.

He attended the Mount Sinai School of Medicine from 2005 until 2009 and began his residency at SUNY, and began fellowship training at the Mount Sinai School of Medicine Hospital.

"When we are going through things, we have no idea why they are happening. Most people don't know that there was a time that I was walking on the streets of New York in the rain with shoes filled with water. That taught me how much I could endure and the lesson was to keep going. The significance of those hard times meant more than I ever could have imagined," he says.

The last angel is Neville's wife, Tashi. "She married me before I had anything," he says.

Their marriage also allowed Neville to become a permanent resident of the United States.

"People see who she is and what she has and may think, she's a doctor's wife and is spending his money. No. She worked as hard as I did, and, along with doing the job of a wife, two parents, and paying the bills, she deserves everything she has and much more," Neville says.

"So much more."

Chapter 7: The Prince of Queens

Next time you see a brother down, stop and pick
him up 'cause you might be the next one stuck.
–Grand Puba, Mind Your Business

In 1965, when Charlie Tucker Sr. purchased a home in Hollis, the east neighborhood of Queens, it was mainly populated by African-American families, but also had a healthy representation of Hispanics, Asians, and West Indians. Having emigrated himself from the Bahamas, it was an ideal place for him and his new wife to settle and raise a family.

Hollis has another distinction that most African Americans of a certain age are well aware of. It was what many consider the birthplace of Hip-hop, although natives of the Boogie Down Bronx might argue the point.

Russell and Joseph Simmons, Darryl McDaniels and Jam Master Jay, the latter three of Run-DMC, were growing up in Hollis in the 60s and 70s, about the same time Charles Tucker Jr. and his older sisters were. So were Jeffrey Atkins, aka Ja Rule, James Todd Smith (LL Cool J.), and Nas.

But, Run-DMC put Hip-hop on the map in the mid-80s and was also the first rap group to be inducted into the Rock and Roll Hall of Fame. They may have also put their hometown on the map nationally and internationally with their homage to their neighborhood in their hit single, "Christmas in Hollis."

The playful rap song tells the story of a kid in Hollis who finds a wallet belonging to Santa Claus and decides to mail the wallet back to him. On Christmas morning, a letter from Santa reveals that all the money inside the wallet was actually intended for the boy.

The optimistic holiday story continues with a hook that describes the happy feelings Christmas time in Hollis stirred up in the members of the group, including home-cooked soul food dinner and lots of gifts under the tree.

But Charles Tucker Jr. describes a different kind of Christmas memory in his hometown.

His parents were both very hard workers and money was tight, especially when it came to him. Maybe it was because he was the only son, and boys aren't meant to be spoiled, he reasons now. But if there was ever any extra money it went to the girls in his family.

When Charles was nine years old, he remembers needing money. He got a job as a paper boy, which required having a bicycle, so his older sister handed him down a yellow girl's Stingray. That wasn't going to cut it for Charles, so he made a decision right then and there to go to work to buy his own bike.

It may have been what launched his fierce work ethic and competitive spirit that still has not waned.

After six months of delivering papers, Charles entered a contest that rewarded paper boys who signed up the most new customers.

Most kids his age would have gone to friends, relatives, and neighbors, or even relied on their parents to give them leads.

Not Charles.

"I opened the phone book and started calling strangers," he says. And his enterprising spirit didn't end there.

"I also subcontracted one of my sisters to help me."

The sheet they were given to list the names of new customers had 10 spots. Charles and his sister exceeded that number.

"We had 10 pages," he says.

Not only did Charles win the contest in his neighborhood, he'd won for the entire district. His reward was not one, but two Mongoose bikes which he calls the Porsches of bicycles, one black and one silver.

Charles continued to deliver newspapers with a daily routine of working for an hour before heading to school each day, and his hard work was paying off.

But when Charles' dad recognized that his son

was beginning to prosper, he demanded a slice of the pie. As Charles tells the story, it was more than a slice.

"My dad started charging me rent, and I was 11 years old! I turned all my money over to him at first, but then I started skimming from the top."

Charles says he kept his hefty tip money for himself, hiding it in his sneakers.

He became a small-time loan shark too, charging his family members five dollars for a regular loan and ten if the loan was over $50.

Charles wasn't making these decisions because he was petty or greedy. He says his parents had no intentions of providing anything other than the basics for him. And he simply had to look out for himself.

"At Christmas time, my sisters would get coats and shoes, and there was nothing for me," he says.

"I started buying my own gifts and putting them under the tree, 'To Charles, from Santa.'"

As he began to earn more money, he also began to develop his own sense of style and soon had the desire to have things he could never have expected from his mom and dad.

By the time he turned 14, Charles was sporting Bally sneakers, an expensive brand highly coveted by the Hip-hop generation of the 80s, especially on the East Coast.

"I went to high school with a Louis Vuitton brief case," Charles says, which may be why he called out Neville Campbell's Louis accessories upon their first meeting.

Part of Charles' style would come from a bus driver and basketball coach named Rick who became a big brother figure to him in his teen years. Charles says Rick knew that his dad was older and stepped in to teach him some things about becoming a young man in New York.

"He was a meticulous dresser when he was off work," Charles says.

But Charles also took notice of the way Rick carried himself and the way he communicated with women.

He had a nice smooth style and there was none of that "yo baby" stuff.

Charles says when he bought his first nice car, he brought it to Rick's house to show him because his opinion was important.

"He was different than a lot of men I had known back then. He never complained about having to go to work like a lot of guys his age I knew. He wasn't always talking about being broke, either. He had a home and that showed me that if you did an honest job and handled your money right, you could live well and have nice things," Charles says.

Rick had many of the same traits regarding work and family his father had, but coming from someone closer to his age, it had more of an impact on Charles at the time.

Rick also did something his dad would never do. He took Charles to his first club, Manhattan Proper, when he was just 17 years old.

These types coming-of-age moments stay with us, especially when adults gain the trust and the admiration from us as teens still determining who we will become in this world. When Charles got older, he says he and Rick had a falling out. But that doesn't erase what he poured into Charles when he had the chance.

"Rick encouraged me to do well in school and always checked up on me. He didn't have to take the time to do that, but he did."

By observing Rick, Charles learned that you don't dress for where you are, you dress for where you are going.

Charles didn't know it yet, but where he was heading was for a life of blessings, love and prosperity. It wouldn't come easily, though.

It rarely does.

After a very successful career as a night manager at the grocery store that employed both his parents, Charles headed off to college. He had hoped to go away to school as his sisters had, but instead, he enrolled in St. John's University, not far from their home in Queens. It is also where Charles would earn his undergraduate, master's, and law degrees.

Charles' keen eye for fashion began to pay off, too. One of the places that employed him as he worked his way through school was a clothing store where he would meet another mentor.

Having a paper route as a kid had turned Charles into a life-long news junkie, and one of his favorite newspaper columnists was a Black sports writer named Rob Parker. Rob, a Queens native, was the first Black sports columnist at the Detroit Free Press and the first Black general columnist at Newsday New York.

"Rob stood out to me because he wasn't afraid to write whatever was on his mind. Even back in the 80s he was bold enough to call Yankees heroes Mickey Mantle and Babe Ruth bums in comparison to Jackie Robinson and Willie Mays," Charles says. "I was impressed by that."

Rob became one of Charles' best customers at the clothing store. Before long, they became close and Rob invited Charles to join his circle of high-profile friends and colleagues. From playing on the paper's softball team to attending the wedding of NBA Hall of Famer Joe Dumars, Charles suddenly had access to events and people who would normally be far out of his reach.

"My first year of law school I was on a plane headed from New York to the NBA All-Star Game in Cleveland along with passengers like Bill Murray and Eddie Murphy," Charles says.

"There I was with my little disposable camera meeting my heroes from the Yankees and the Knicks and even Brandy!"

But what Charles loved the most was the chance to sit in the press box at the game and meet Black editors from across the nation, like Garry D. Howard who wrote for the Philadelphia Enquirer and later the

Associated Press and the late Bryan Burwell from the St. Louis Dispatch and USA Today.

"To see a collective unit of Black editors who shaped journalism and sports all supporting each other blew me away."

Rubbing elbows with the movers and shakers taught Charles lessons about loyalty, too. He once attended a Christmas party at Rob Parker's house where two of the guests included a then up-and-coming young Philadelphia sportswriter named Stephen A. Smith and his homeboy, NBA star Allen Iverson.

Years later, Parker would debate Stephen A. Smith and co-host Skip Bayless on Smith's hit ESPN sports program "First Take."

Eventually, one of the things about Rob Parker that Charles admired most got him into trouble.

Rob was suspended for remarking that Washington Redskins quarterback Robert Griffin III wasn't Black enough. The controversy did not end his career, but it definitely was a bad moment for him.

Charles thought that Stephen A. Smith could have done more to help out the man who looked out for him before Stephen A. became a famous journalist and broadcaster.

"Rob played a role in Stephen A.'s success back in the day and I don't think Stephen A. had his back," Charles says.

That incident solidified for Charles an example of how you can make a difference in someone's life behind the scenes without ever getting recognition for it.

After his contract was not renewed at ESPN, Rob joined a rival sports show, "Skip and Shannon: Undisputed," on Fox Sports.

"He continued to do well, but I never liked the turn his career took back then. I would have liked to have seen more of the people that Rob helped when he was up reach out to him when he was down."

Perhaps that is why Charles is so intentional about mentioning the two men from his hometown, Rick and Rob, who took the time to take him under their wings in two very different ways.

"I'll always remember both of them," he says.

Chapter 8: Rebel with a Cause

Everything negative is an opportunity
for me to rise. –Kobe Bryant

F. Travis Buchanan is a self-proclaimed basketball fanatic. So much so that in 1989 the Phineas Banning High School senior would make his final choice of which college to attend based on the winner of a basketball tournament.

The University of Arizona was his original choice, but the ultimate decision lay in the outcome of the NCAA third-round tournament where the first-place Arizona Wildcats were poised to defeat the University of Nevada's Runnin' Rebels.

The Rebels, loaded with talent, were led by controversial head coach, Jerry Tarkanian. But they were less experienced than the Wildcats, and, because of their on-the-court aggressive play and off-the-court swagger, many people wrote them off.

Being written off was certainly a concept Travis could relate to.

"We had white teachers in high school who would discourage the Black students from doing high-level things," Travis says.

"I remember an English teacher telling our class that none of us would ever have anything published. I wasn't influenced by that type of negativity, but some kids probably were and decided that they would never be anything because of it."

Like many suburban schools, Travis' high school, located in Wilmington, California experienced a racial shift during the 60s and 70s as more Black and Brown families moved to his hometown of Carson that borders the city of Wilmington. Some educators were not as prepared as others to meet the needs of students from varying backgrounds.

Back in 1975, before Travis arrived, a college guidance counselor at the high school reportedly noted that only 30 of the school's 1,200 tenth graders were in honors classes and only five percent of the graduates were going to college. She and a fellow counselor introduced a college core curriculum open to all students but on a contractual basis. They had to pledge to complete a minimum amount of study time per day, and have no more than five absences per semester.

By the third year of the program 1,100 students were enrolled.

But some teachers complained about having to teach students who traditionally would not be accepted into college-prep type programs. However, some of the students who would have originally been screened out went on to become successful college students.

Travis didn't fall into the category of being poverty stricken or having a lack of positive role models in life. His father was a successful corporate executive and he grew up in an upper middle-class suburban home. He also had the grades to get accepted into college. Still, the negative comment from that teacher stuck with him.

"When someone tells me I can't do something or I'm met with a challenge, it makes me want to succeed even more," Travis says.

On March 23, 1989, University of Nevada-Las Vegas faced Arizona in the Western Regional semi-finals, and, thanks to the pact Travis made with himself, his future hung in the balance.

Travis says either school would have been fine for him, but his main goal was to get out of Los Angeles and be close enough to drive home. Both Tucson and Las Vegas were less than an eight-hour drive away from his dad's home in Carson.

The game was close from the opening moments up until the final buzzer-beating shot.

At half time the score was 38-37 with UNLV in the lead. The last player to score in the second half was Runnin' Rebel's star guard, Anderson Hunt. UNLV defeated Arizona, 68-67, sealing Travis' fate.

Travis entered the University of Nevada Las Vegas in the fall of 1989 and received a Bachelor of Science degree from its Lee College of Business in

1992. He went on to receive his JD from Western State College of Law in Los Angeles.

"Law school was difficult and challenging," Travis concedes. "But I loved it. It was the hardest I've ever worked," he says.

Graduating from law school was a major accomplishment, but taking the infamous California State Bar Exam proved to be grueling.

What makes it more difficult to pass than other bar exams is that the State of California has the second highest pass score in the country, 144. The national median score needed to pass the bar is 135.

Some studies say between 34 percent and 61 percent of African Americans fail the California Bar Exam the first time around and before Travis got his results, he had already prepared himself for the worst.

"I had my speech ready for why I didn't pass," Travis says.

"Thankfully, I didn't have to use it."

Knowing the odds were against him passing the bar his first try did not have an impact on Travis' score, but for many African Americans and women, that is not the case. For some, the systems and institutions have a way of damaging their self-esteem by inadvertently reminding them of an expectation of under-achievement. The statistics tell the story, but professors, counselors, and mentors can help buffer students from the negative numbers and help them concentrate on succeeding against the odds.

The basketball coach of the Runnin' Rebels at

Travis' alma mater UNLV taught his players to play "weak-side defense," a strategy that allows a player to help teammates out on the other side of the court, away from the ball. That is the kind of mentoring that is needed for many people of color.

The students are carrying the ball, but without having help beside them, it is difficult to have the follow-through needed to be successful.

Weak-side defense requires a combination of communication and being at the right spot at the right time.

Travis passed the bar and has been on a winning streak ever since, first becoming a prosecutor in the Los Angeles City Attorney's office, and then going on to represent the privately run Department of Water and Power. He distinguished himself by becoming the first ever to promote from within the city's criminal law entity to Water and Power. From there, he joined the Los Angeles Unified School District's legal department and, after being selected from a pool of 300 applicants, he was promoted to general counsel of L.A. Unified, the largest school district in the country. That position brought Travis a bit of additional pride and joy. His old high school, Banning, was part of that school district and he wonders what would have happened if he had let his teacher's doubts about him get into his head.

But like the Runnin' Rebels of 1989, he never lets the naysayers get to him.

"I proved her wrong," he says.

Chapter 9: The Turning Point

If you can't change it, change your attitude.
—Maya Angelou

Each of us have moments in our lives that seem to define the path we will take. They can stem from uplifting words of compassion or hurtful events that have shaken us to our core.

When Neville was a young boy growing up in Jamaica, he believed that his parents favored him less because of the dark color of his skin. His older brother, who was lighter skinned, was always positively viewed in comparison.

Neville says his family's views were just a reflection of the way many Jamaicans felt.

"In our country, the lighter-skinned people were always in the forefront in offices and stores."

Neville says he felt bad as a child because he was never treated as well as his brother was. He knew his parents were showing favoritism, but he was surprised to discover that someone else recognized it too.

"One day a neighbor who we called Aunt

Carmen pulled me aside and said something that I will never forget," he says.

"She said, 'I would like you to know that you are a beautiful creation.' Then she told me to look her in the eyes and she repeated those words four or five times and added, 'You are no less than anyone else.' I cried," Neville says.

"In that moment, it was like a switch went on and I realized that who I was on the inside needed to shine."

That brief encounter changed the way Neville saw himself and was the confidence booster the young boy needed in that moment.

"The next day, you couldn't tell me anything!" he says.

Even though eight-year-old Charles didn't have many extended family members in the States, he did have an uncle whom the family would see from time to time. Because this uncle was on the younger side, Charles considered him to be someone he could relate to and developed a closeness to him.

But Charles said an early morning incident changed the way he would look at this uncle.

As the family was preparing to leave for one of their family vacations to Florida, Charles and one of his sisters found their uncle passed out on the backyard steps, Charles recalls, still unable to hide the disillusionment in his voice.

"We thought he was dead," he says.

It turned out that his uncle was in a drunken stupor, and Charles' mom and dad were so upset about the spectacle he had made, they insisted that he leave right away. But seeing his beloved uncle that way broke Charles' heart.

"I was so disappointed in him," he says. "It was just a very poor example of a man and I knew after that I didn't want to emulate him in any way."

Even at one of Phillip's lowest points after being arrested and forced to leave law school, he had one bright spot in his life, his little brother. Barely making a living and uncertain about his future, Phillip still made room for Todd because he couldn't risk the chance of him getting into trouble.

"I was working at Vitamin World in a dying mall in Jacksonville, Florida," he says. "My little brother was supposed to go to the Navy but that didn't work out, so he stayed with me."

Phillip says what could have been a burdensome time turned out to be fabulous for the both of them.

"We were living together on our own for almost three years, and as hard as it was financially, it felt good having him there because I knew it was the best place for him to be."

Todd remained with Phillip until he got accepted into a correctional officer's program in Gainesville, Florida. He completed that program and has gone on to build a career with multiple promotions, and he is now a federal corrections officer in Miami.

Too many young people are left on their own because they're old enough to be a success, but for most of us, we need someone to hold on to us and see us through hard times.

"That's what I tried to do for my little brother and I couldn't be more proud of him," Phillip says, sounding almost like a dad praising an accomplished son. The richness of their relationship goes deeper, though.

"Looking back, I needed him just as much as he needed me."

For years, Travis believed he was his father's only son, but at age nine he discovered his father had another son a year and a half older than he was. It was a surprise that Travis had trouble processing at the time.

"I was jealous of my half bother," he says. "I didn't like the attention he got from my dad."

The hardest part was that Travis' new brother seemed to have special status without having earned it, in his nine-year-old eyes.

"He popped up from nowhere and all of a sudden my dad was all over him."

It turned out Travis had nothing to be jealous about. His relationship with his dad continued to get stronger as Travis grew older, and for much of that time, his brother was hardly in the picture. But when their dad got ill years later, Travis was happy to see his dad and brother reconnect.

75

"It was good for both of them to be in each other's lives, especially at that point," Travis says.

"I wanted them to get to know each other. I had my dad all of my life and now his time was coming to an end. I felt like, please, have your time with him."

The unselfish gesture Travis was making was a sign of his maturity as well as the security in knowing that nothing or no one could replace what he and his father shared. It was fine for his brother to establish his own relationship with their father.

Even though Travis and his brother eventually established a good relationship of their own, he says he feels closer to Carlos, Charles, Neville, and Phillip than he does with anyone outside of his immediate family.

"The five of us have bonded," he says. "These are the brothers I never had."

Things happen for a reason, Carlos says. God is constantly working in our lives without us knowing the plans he has for our future. And the timing of his divine intervention is impeccable.

When Carlos' mom made the $35,000 investment into his dream of opening up a private law practice, he used a portion of it to buy a BMW his wife Natalie's dad found for him. The first time Carlos was scheduled to drive their two-year-old daughter, Avery, to daycare, he did the unthinkable. He forgot to drop her off and drove straight to his law office. In three to five minutes, an alarm notified

Carlos that someone was in his car. Immediately, he remembered that he had failed to drop off his baby girl and rushed out to retrieve her from the car.

"If it had not been for that alarm…it breaks my heart to even imagine what would have happened to my daughter," Carlos says. "I am so blessed that that feature was on the car."

Carlos eventually became a blessing to another man who had the same kind of lapse as he did by leaving his toddler in a vehicle, only this man's story had a horrific ending.

"When I heard about a guy in Grenada, Mississippi who was arrested and taken to jail after his daughter died in the backseat of his car, I knew he was not a negligent or abusive parent," Carlos says.

"He forgot, and, if it hadn't happened to me, I probably would have cast the same type of judgement on him that most people had."

Carlos represented the distraught father pro-bono.

"The prosecutor wanted to have him put away for murder and for fear of going to prison, he took a felony plea," Carlos says.

"That was my most memorable case because I could easily put myself in his place. When I saw him on the news screaming and hollering over losing his child, I knew that could have been me."

In Carlos' mind, God set it up for him to go through it first so that he could reach out to the father who needed someone to understand his pain and his predicament.

"I'm still in touch with him after all these years," Carlos says.

The former client and his wife went on to have twin boys.

"God had a blessing in store for him after all."

Chapter 10: Legacy

To know the road ahead, ask those coming back.
–Chinese proverb

We can all look back at our lives and recognize things we would have done differently if we'd had the chance. But would we be willing to forfeit the valuable lessons we learned along the way?

The Five Brothers can all testify to the growth and the glory that has resulted from some of their most trying experiences. But they are also advocates of helping others steer clear of certain types of adversity when possible, especially Phillip, who is the youngest of the Five. He is a strong believer of helping those you care about avoid pitfalls at any cost.

"If you want someone to be great, you have to see them through the rough times," he says emphatically.

"Every time you get one person over the hill, you go back and bring someone else along," he says.

Phillip's words are backed up by what he feels he may have missed out on, coupled with the way he is now mentoring his siblings that include two younger sisters. The nurturing that children require doesn't end when they turn 18 or even 21, he says.

"I need to stick with you until you become great."

The responsibility we have to each other, especially in the African-American community, reaches beyond bloodlines, the Brothers contend.

Both Phillip and Charles share similar stories about potential mentors who they feel did not do their parts when the opportunities presented themselves.

"There are people who looked like us and knew the struggles we were having but still wouldn't help," Charles says, referring to a particular gentleman who could have played a positive role in his life.

There was a Black attorney in the community who Charles knew as a teen who watched him as he progressed through college and also knew that Charles was in law school. Yet he would never so much as have a conversation with him back then. Charles finds this behavior indefensible.

"He could have offered me money or books or even offered me a job." Charles speaks as though he still cannot believe the disinterest the attorney showed in him. It was a missed opportunity to contribute to someone traveling on your path. Why wouldn't you?

Phillip can relate.

He remembers being a teacher's assistant for a professor and doing a very good job. He says that experience taught him how he did not want to treat others.

"Individuals going through college and law school should be aware of the way the game is often played," Phillip says. It's something he had no clue about at the time.

"I believed you enter things with your best foot forward and that you reap what you sow. That was my motivation while working for the professors."

But he got a rude awakening when it appeared that his efforts would not pay off the way he hoped they would.

Phillip says he noticed that the closer you get to the time when the people with power have to make a decision about your future, the more cautious they are of you.

"It's easy to take on a first-year intern in law school because there are three years between that day and the time he or she will ask for a job," he explains.

"But when you're almost to the end, it's expected that you will be asking for a job and that's something some professors want to avoid."

Phillip says he worked very hard with the expectation that he would be rewarded. In fact, he says, it was more than an expectation, there was a real promised job opportunity pledged to encourage him to go above and beyond what was required.

"The professor was a wealthy, well-connected man who could have helped me get my foot in the door. Why would you let someone go through all of that?"

Phillip had proven to be an asset as a research

assistant and wrote several projects and articles that were published on behalf of this mentor that advanced his career.

In the meantime, Phillip had created a scrolling technology that had won the attention of Major League Baseball. He had an ambitious plan of using that relationship to gain a position in MLB's general counsel's office. It didn't work out, but Phillip says he did it on his own with no one leading him. His mentor's support could have been invaluable; however, it just wasn't there.

Luckily, someone will gain from those kinds of opportunities Phillip and Charles may have lost.

Due to the oversights and ways that students are sometimes used and manipulated by the system, without any real compensation, the Five Brothers are determined to step in when they see young Black attorneys and doctors who can use a helping hand.

It might not always be with money, or a job offer, but sometimes through support, exposure, and access to something that will be meaningful to their lives and careers. The Brothers are intentional about living their version of the Golden Rule.

"We will do for others what we wish others had done for us," Charles says.

Phillip says when the Brothers heard his story about possibly losing his opportunity of becoming a lawyer, they went to work to try to expedite the time it would take for him to receive the clearance he needs to be made whole in the eyes of the American Bar Association.

"Some of what I needed was money that no one I knew was able or willing to give me. It was $4,000. If I had $4,000 back then, I could have been in a different place today," he says.

When Carlos met Phillip, he saw something in him that others didn't see, and brought him into the fold.

"Phillip is relentless and fearless," Carlos says. "Despite what he's been through, he keeps going forward."

Travis agrees and says Phillip gave them all a chance to influence him in a positive way. He says having an attorney to mentor him in his youth would have been helpful.

"We didn't have that when we were young. No one who looked like me tried to take me under their wing."

However, God doesn't make mistakes, Neville says, and he believes everything they each went through was orchestrated in order for them to enjoy a harmonious relationship that blesses them and others, too.

"He brought us all together in the last five years and has navigated this whole situation," Neville says.

"If Phillip had gotten the $4,000 he needed right away, his story might have been a lot different. Years down the line, the significance of the five of us meeting could become more than any of us could have envisioned."

Each of the Brothers have achieved a respectable amount of success individually and still have higher hopes for the future in regard to themselves, their offspring, and their siblings. As important as it is to be a good role model to those they meet on a professional level, they also recognize that their most important work begins with who they are influencing at home.

Carlos has his eye set on going into politics and possibly becoming the first Black governor of Mississippi. In the meantime, he continues to fight the good fight trying civil rights cases and giving power to the powerless by representing families in wrongful death suits. As a husband to Natalie and father to Avery Nicole, Carlos has every reason to strive to make his city, his state, and his country better and safer places he can be proud of.

Charles not only is excited about ways to give back, he is grateful for what he is still receiving from elders, and in particular his wife LaDonna's father who pastors a church. He believes the example his in-laws have set as a loving couple and as loving parents, as well as the way they have welcomed him in the family with open arms, have made him a better man. Charles himself has completed training to become a minister and with his father-in-law and mother-in-law's blessings he will become head pastor of their church someday.

It is a tall order that Charles humbly accepts. His

walk as a Christian takes priority in his life as a father to his three children, as a husband, and as a professional, because he believes that everything he does is influenced by his belief in and commitment to Christ.

In fact, all five of the Brothers speak openly and boldly about their spirituality; what it has meant to them as children, and now as men serving in their present careers, and even as they look toward their future.

Travis, who has aspirations of ending his career as a judge, says he can see himself winding down and away from daily law practice in five years or so.

"I've been practicing for 23 years and it has been better than I could have imagined," he says. "Every five years or so, I've taken a leap of faith because I've never wanted to get too comfortable or stop challenging myself," he says.

As fathers, Neville, Carlos, Charles, and Travis now have an added incentive for keeping their legacy of excellence going. They all share common concerns as they struggle to make sure their children understand their own responsibility of working hard and giving back.

"Their lives are so different than ours were," Carlos says. "We all have to figure out how to make sure we aren't giving them too much."

They all agree that there has to a balance

between providing material things their children want versus providing the necessities.

As parents and as humans, we have the tendency to do more for our children than our parents were able to do for us. But that often comes with a cost. The importance of learning tough lessons, making sacrifices, and even struggling at times has a place in each of the Brothers' success. Figuring out that balance is something foremost on their minds. Unlike law and medicine, there are no advanced degrees in parenting your own children.

Each of the Brothers grew up with parents who have poured into them in some ways good or bad, and they have made the decision of choosing which portions they will pass on to their offspring. They concede that even when their own mothers and fathers fell short, they all were giving it the best they had.

Neville has three daughters, 18-year-old Tashell; Giselle, 11; and Gabrielle, who is 9.

His biggest hope is to teach all three to respect and value the relationships they have with other people, and to learn what to say and what not to say.

"I learned from my mom to walk into a room and without saying a word to know who is sad, who is troubled, and which one needs help right away," he says.

That technique works in the medical profession and at home with his family. Neville says keeping his finger on the pulse of their emotions is crucial to his relationships with his girls.

Travis is concerned about the lack of time available for him and his wife, Carla, an assistant principal, to spend with their two daughters, Lauren, 18, and Sydney, 16, as they maneuver through life as busy professionals.

"I feel so guilty about being in their lives as a provider but not present enough day to day. I'm trying to find that balance, and it has been a personal challenge," he says.

Travis even wonders if the effort he's making now is happening too late.

"I'm trying to give our girls one-on-one time and they don't really want it anymore. They're teenagers with their own schedules and plans," he says.

Charles and his wife LaDonna have two daughters, Cassidy, 12 and Londyn, 10, and a son, Charles Tucker III, (Lil Charles) who is 8. He says his most important job as a father is to train his children to have a relationship with Christ in spirit and in truth, building on what he has gotten as a minister and what he has learned growing up in church.

Charles says when he looks at his son, he wonders if his own dad looked at him with the same joy and overwhelming sense of pride.

"Charles III has such a compassionate heart and he is genuinely a good kid," he says, choking up as he describes his only boy.

"His thoughts are not to harm anyone, he enjoys learning, and he is constantly thinking. To know that I actually had something to do with that is amazing to me."

Charles realizes that children grow and change and he's preparing himself for those days, too. Thinking back to his own childhood, he says he hopes his relationships with his children are not needlessly combative the way his sometimes were with his own father.

"I'm striving for a closer relationship," he says.

Phillip is single with no children but has played a major role in his younger brother Todd's life. He hopes to be able to have a similar impact with his little sister who is currently a college student. But he's also looking ahead to when he has children of his own. His goal is to always be in the position of giving his children whatever help they need regardless of what stage they're in.

"I want my ceiling to be their floor," Phillip says.

The contacts he's made, the access to people he knows, and the understanding of the things that aren't written in books will work in his children's favor when he has them.

"I would want them working right here (The Cochran Firm) as an intern," he says.

The Five Brothers are all extremely proud to be part of The Cochran Firm and consider Johnnie L.

Cochran a role model in spite of the fact that they've never personally met the legendary attorney. They do, however, know what he stood for.

Travis was born and raised in the Los Angeles area and may have had the best sense of who Johnnie Cochran was, even before much of the rest of the world knew.

"He was already a legend in L.A. before he blew up around the country with the O.J. trial," Travis says.

Supreme Court Justice Thurgood Marshall's victory in the Brown vs. The Board of Education case inspired Cochran to pursue a career in law. He passed the bar exam in 1963, and in 1966 he opened his own law practice. By 1970, he had established himself as the premier litigator for high profile police brutality cases.

In 1978, Johnnie Cochran joined the L.A. District Attorney's office and later returned to private practice, forming The Cochran Firm in 1983. His name was heard frequently on local news when he represented Black college football player Ron Settles' family in a wrongful death suit against the police. Cochran won the family close to a million dollars, a huge sum in the early 1980s. By the time Cochran was hired by O.J. Simpson, his legal prowess had been demonstrated and he was well known and well regarded.

In 1997, Cochran teamed up with a group of attorneys and The Cochran Firm expanded into a national law firm with more than 30 regional offices across the country, including Los Angeles, Dallas, Chicago, Atlanta, and Baltimore. Headquartered in Dothan, Alabama, the firm concentrates mainly on civil cases and fulfills Cochran's dream of bringing attorneys of diverse ethnic backgrounds to work together to provide legal representation for injured people.

Johnnie Cochran passed away in 2005.

Charles says Cochran was definitely a role model.

"He prided himself on being an excellent trial attorney, had a phenomenal level of preparedness, and there was always the understanding that the cases he tried were bigger than he was. He was very forward thinking."

Being part of his firm is a true representation of the kind of Black excellence in which Charles and the others take so much pride.

Neville, who grew up in Jamaica, says he was impressed with the way Cochran was able to win the O.J. Simpson case with so many odds against him. "He argued it with brilliance," he says.

What people fail to accept is, whether you agree with the Simpson verdict or not, Johnnie Cochran used his skills to establish the reasonable doubt needed to bring about an acquittal. And he also called attention to racism within law enforcement that was very real in Los Angeles and surrounding areas. Cochran was not afraid to play the "race card," something much of mainstream America and media found to be distasteful.

Carlos followed in Johnnie Cochran's footsteps by also becoming known for taking on police brutality and wrongful death suits in Mississippi, along with law partner Charles.

Carlos also joined the same college fraternity as Cochran, Kappa Alpha Psi.

"He was my biggest inspiration for joining because I wanted to be like him in every way," Carlos says.

"I'm now living my wildest dream being a partner in the law firm founded by him.

"Wow! Just Wow!"

* * * * *

Reflections

On Discipline

Got my first paddling in first grade, probably being disrespectful. If I got in trouble at school, I got in trouble at home. My mom would give me more licks but they were soft, my dad's were fewer but harder.
—Carlos

Mom's level of discipline with the daughters is different than it was with ours. She's definitely softer with them than she was with us. Anything I said to my mom, she said I was raising my voice. I was just trying to respond. In her mind, everything she did was for the greater good.
—Phillip

On Work and Money

I got my strong work ethic from my dad. I started cutting grass at the age of 7. I always assisted him no matter what. I would use the money I made to buy ice cream sandwiches and sell them to my sister for 25 cents.
—Carlos

My first job was KFC at age 16. Before that, I used to get an allowance of $20 a week in high school and I would save up to get Christmas and back-to-school clothes. If you close the store, you have to clean the chicken grease. Nobody knew what time KFC closed, so I had a side hustle selling the chicken after hours. I was getting $50 extra. That was $500 a week in high school besides my paycheck. We became the most efficient KFC, but

eventually, I told them what was happening after hours. My boss said, congrats, you're going to be fired.
—Phillip

My brother and I had pigs, cows, chicken and goats to tend to. After, we did our housework. We had 12 or 15 pens to wash out.
—Neville

I worked at McDonald's and got fired. A customer cussed me out because it took too long for him to get his fries. I had words for him.
—Travis

Mom and Dad worked at the same grocery store and got me a job there. I pushed carts for a week and became a cashier. I took training and at 18 became a front manager. I started making $28,000 a year as a night manager and started re-thinking law school. At one time, I was selling vacuum cleaners when I came home from school. Apartment buildings were a challenge because nobody wanted to go to them, but I would. The goal was three sales a week, I would get 9 or 10.
—Charles

On Love

I was going to marry my college sweetheart but I called it off eight weeks before the wedding. It was one of the hardest things I ever did. Six weeks later I met my wife. It was meant to be.
—Carlos

I believed in love at first sight. I knew my wife was the one, no doubt. After meeting her in Florida, I went back to NY and cleared the bench. I felt like I had caught the big fish and had to find a way to reel her in.
—Charles

Most people don't know what my wife has done for me.
—Neville

On Family

I loved watching my grandmother age. She was cool but she was so mean to my friends. She died in my freshman year of high school, but before that, I helped my mom, take care of her. It was special. But to see all that my mom went through in her 30s is strange because I'm close to that age now.
—Phillip

My wife's family is so loving. It's one of the first things I noticed about them. We were a close family but it was a different kind of closeness. My wife's family is touchy-feely. If I see her today, she hugs me like I haven't seen her for six months.
—Charles

Carlos is a Kappa and I'm an Alpha. My wife is an AKA. The Alphas were my family who supported me through college and told me I would be the man one day.
—Travis

I try to make it a point to tell my children I love them. I was correcting my son last night and I raised my voice. I called him and apologized. There were no apologies from my dad.
—Charles

We always had a gathering of boys and girls coming to play, partly because there was always food. My mother made sure of it.
—Neville

On Travel

If we got good grades we would go to Red Lobster or a weekend trip. Disney World in the summer. We would also go on vacations to New Orleans or somewhere could drive to. I took my first flight at age 16 to Czechoslovakia as part of my school's global education exchange. It inspired me to travel more and I've been to the Caribbean, Canada, Mexico, Africa, Paris, and South America. I still want to go to Asia and Australia.
—Carlos

I thought that Days Inn was as nice as it got. I didn't get on a plane until I was in college. We'd go on road trips. We'd leave at 3 or 4 in the morning. If my dad said we were leaving at 3, we were leaving at 3. One time, we drove off and I realized we had left the cooler at home with our Kool Aid. We said, "We need our Kool Aid!" My dad said, "I will cool your ass and give you Aid." He kept driving.
—Charles

The Five Brothers

On Disappointment

I never had failed a class until I got to college and failed physics. I cried because I had failed for the first time in my life. I had a semester to pull it together and get my GPA up. I changed my major to political science.
—Carlos

My older sisters dominated my life. My parents made sure I had the basics—a coat, pair of shoes. Anything extra I had to wait for hand me downs from sisters. Up until the age of 9 when it started getting embarrassing.
—Charles

After college graduation, I realized life was about to get real.
—Phillip

On Wisdom

The fears that you have now will be your greatest strengths in the future. Lot of fears, doubts, and questions inhibited me from being the best me. This is who you are and why you are unique, own it. Once I understood that, doors started opening.
—Neville

This too shall pass. Just keep pushing through.
—Charles

Every time you get one person over the hill, you go back and bring someone else along. If you tell me you want to be great, I need to stick with you until you become great.
—Phillip

If a challenge seems insurmountable, take it and prove people wrong. I was destined to be a lawyer. Even though there were times that I thought I couldn't do it, I went for it and it worked out.
—Travis

Mary Flowers Boyce was the Head Writer for the nationally syndicated Tom Joyner Morning Show and co-author of Joyner's memoir, *I'm Just a D.J., but It Makes Sense to Me*. She is also a contributor in the best-selling anthology: *Shift: Twenty Women Share Stories of Strength, Courage, and Succeeding Against the Odds*.

Born in Chicago, Illinois, she was raised in Compton, California, and currently resides in Dallas, Texas with her husband and sometimes their two amazing young adults.

Made in the USA
Middletown, DE
20 December 2020